The Ultimate Sunflower Book

The Ultimate Sunflower Book

Lucy Peel

HarperCollins*Publishers*

NOTES ON THE RECIPES
- Use medium eggs unless otherwise stated.
- Spoon measurements are level unless otherwise stated.
- Imperial and metric measurements have been calculated separately, so follow one set of measurements within a recipe.

First published in the United States of America in 1997 by HarperCollins*Publishers*, New York

Text © Lucy Peel

For HarperCollins*Publishers*:

Editorial Director: Polly Powell
Editor and Picture Researcher: Becky Humphreys
Senior Designer: Clare Baggaley
Photographer: Laura Wickenden
Indexer: Sue Bosanko

A CIP catalogue for this book is available from the Library of Congress

First edition
10 9 8 7 6 5 4 3 2 1

ISBN 0-06-270212-2

Reproduction by United Graphic Pte Ltd

Printed and bound by Graficas Estella, Spain

Contents

Sunflowers as inspiration: a history

Sunflowers have been a popular image since the Aztec era. Across the world, they have been adopted as a symbol of light, hope and innocence. The inspiration of artists for centuries, sunflowers are now everywhere, defying the seasons as they stare jauntily out at us from hundreds of products such as T-shirts, cards, posters and from all kinds of advertisements.

The most cheerful flower in the world

You cannot open a magazine or newspaper without seeing the bright, open face of a sunflower. Every photograph of a celebrity's home — be it an English country cottage, a French château or an ultra-modern condo in America's Hollywood Hills — features a vase of sunflowers gracing a table. Numerous companies, anxious to share a bit of the buzz associated with this delightful flower, have adopted it as their logo, and use it in advertisements to create a feeling of youth and vigor.

What is it about the humble sunflower (*Helianthus annuus*) that so delights us and has made them so fabulously fashionable? Is it the bright, open flowers with their ever-cheerful faces turned up to the sun? Or is it the sunflower's sheer stature? Maybe it is simply that the sunflower is so beautiful, yet so useful, and that it captures the very essence of summer – clear blue skies and the warmth of the life-giving sun. Across the world the sunflower has been adopted as a symbol of light, hope and innocence. It is truly a flower for all people – young and old, artist and artisan.

SUNFLOWERS AS INSPIRATION

Sunflowers have inspired painters and poets throughout the centuries. Van Gogh and Gauguin could not resist their vibrancy. So much so that in the late 1880s the former set up a studio in Provence where he painted sunflowers again and again, trying to capture their vibrant magic. More recently, David Hockney has exhibited sunflower paintings.

The poet William Blake perceived a curious melancholy behind the sunflower's cheeriness, while the painter John Piper loved them so much that when he died in 1992, a carving of a sunflower was chosen for his gravestone.

THEY'RE NOT JUST YELLOW!

Although everyone knows what a sunflower is, the image they invariably call to mind is the bright

yellow of the common sunflower – the *Helianthus annuus*. In fact, there are countless varieties and the number is growing every year. As the sunflower becomes increasingly popular as a decorative motif, demand for the real thing has soared. Plant breeders have responded to this demand by developing a host of new varieties in every size and color imaginable. So while catalogs and documents from the last century list only a handful of varieties, now the sunflower family can boast more than a hundred, with glorious names such as 'Velvet Queen', 'Golden Globe' and 'Lion's Mane'.

Although most sunflowers are the yellow you would expect, the blooms also come in shades of golden-orange, sizzling red and mellow brown. There are perennials as well as annuals, and summer- as well as autumn-flowering varieties. And not all sunflowers are immensely tall. There are dwarfs as well as giants, and double as well as single varieties.

USEFUL AS WELL AS BEAUTIFUL

But the sunflower is more than an ornamental plant. Behind its beauty there lies a strong streak of practicality. Every part of it can be put to use, as the native peoples of the Americas discovered many thousands of years ago. They domesticated the sunflower, cultivating it for oil, food, medicine and dye. With the arrival of European settlers, traders and adventurers, sunflowers soon found their way to Western Europe, and from there to Russia. It was in Russia that their potential was realized. Thousands of acres were planted and many new strains and varieties were developed.

Today sunflowers are big business. When the seeds are crushed, they yield a very pure oil which is excellent for cooking and makes delicious margarine. Surprisingly, this oil is also used in the chemical and plastics industries. Sunflower seeds are a key ingredient in bird and pet food mixes, as well as being eaten by humans in salads, in casseroles or simply as

Stan Herd planted a 220 x 330 yds/200 x 300 m pastiche of Van Gogh's sunflowers near Eudora, Kansas, to commemorate the 125th anniversary of the state.

a snack. The massive demand for their seeds, oil and associated products resulted in many millions of acres being planted across the globe, making sunflowers the world's fifth largest oil-seed crop. Even the pith has been pressed into service in the past – for the manufacture of lifebelts (being an amazing ten times lighter than cork) – while the spent plant is not wasted, but made into silage.

The wonder of sunflower seeds is not just that they are delicious. The glorious thing is that they are packed to bursting with vitamins, minerals and fiber, and are high in linoleic acid – a polyunsaturated fatty acid which actually lowers the level of cholesterol in the blood and reduces the risk of heart disease. So we can not only enjoy the delicious flavors, but feel virtuous eating them.

GARDENING WITH SUNFLOWERS

In the garden sunflowers provide unequalled vibrancy. Their astonishing range of heights and dazzling colors means there is a sunflower to suit any situation, whether it be to provide height at the back of a border, to line a path or frame an entrance. At the other end of the scale, the smaller, bushier varieties make fantastic edging plants and look spectacular in containers.

Sunflowers can be grown as informal hedges, as screens to hide unsightly objects, such as an oil tank or compost heap, and they make the most fantastic focal points. Their height, color and enormous flowers irresistibly draw the eye, distracting from any unsightly areas of the garden.

As an introduction to gardening, sunflowers cannot be beaten. They are guaranteed to give children the gardening bug. Their bright open faces and immense stature brings almost instant results, sunflowers are the perfect first-time plant.

On a practical level, sunflowers are immensely valuable to gardeners as they make excellent companion crops for a variety of vegetables. They also attract a host of beneficial insects to help keep pests at bay.

SUNFLOWERS IN THE HOME

Indoors, sunflowers are so astonishingly versatile that they are a joy for the flower arranger to work with and an inspiration for anyone interested in crafts. They can be made to look grand and opulent, or delightfully simple and informal.

They will brighten up the gloomiest corner, bringing sunshine into the house, and even when their season is over, their magic can still go on working. For when dried or used as the inspiration for a stencil to decorate a room, the warmth and energy of summer can be captured to cheer up even the dullest, grey, winter's day.

THE MOST POPULAR FLOWER IN THE WORLD?

With all these qualities it is no wonder that Kansas has adopted the sunflower as its state flower, and that there is a growing movement throughout the nation to get it recognized as the national flower. It is a magnificent plant which deserves a space in everyone's garden, as well as everyone's larder.

Ah! Sunflower

Ah, Sunflower! weary of time,
Who countest the steps of the Sun,
Seeking after that sweet golden clime
Where the traveller's journey is done:

Where the Youth pined away with desire,
And the pale Virgin shrouded in snow
Arise from their graves, and aspire
Where my Sunflower wishes to go.

WILLIAM BLAKE

Sunflowers today

The inspiration of artists for centuries, sunflowers are now a key motif for hundreds of contemporary designers.

gardening with sunflowers

The potential for gardening with sunflowers is enormous. They can be used in so many different ways, to create so many different looks, being just as appropriate for informal schemes, as for very formal ones. You could even create a miniature Provençal landscape, with a small sea of swaying sunflower heads.

Planning and preparation

Despite their recent ubiquity as a popular image, sunflowers have historically been neglected by gardeners. They were dismissed as a crop, and therefore considered not worthy of a place in the garden. So, they were consigned to children's gardens, where they were grown as a novelty, or to traditional cottage gardens. This was a shame as the humble sunflower, besides being an extremely nutritious food source (see Cooking with Sunflowers, page 50), and very beautiful, has other properties which make it a valuable asset to a gardener:

✿ Sunflowers grow very quickly; many can put on 6 ft/1.8 m or more, in a season. This is very valuable if you have an eyesore that you want to hide.

✿ Sunflowers are easily cultivated from home-grown seed, so you can have an everlasting supply of sunflowers – a very inexpensive source of color for your garden.

✿ Sunflowers come into their own towards the end of summer when herbaceous plants are dying off, because this is when they come into bloom. Their uplifting, sunny colors really brighten up the garden.

✿ Sunflowers can also act as protectors to other plants, shading shorter plants and shielding their more fragile neighbours from damaging winds.

✿ On top of all of this, sunflowers will inhibit weeds, attract pest-controlling insects and birds, and even act as living supports for other plants.

When planning any garden, it is advisable to start by taking a step back and looking long and hard at the overall picture. This is the time to decide what image you are trying to create, and to identify any specific problems – such as an ugly oil tank which needs disguising. It may be that there is only one bed which needs revamping, in which case you need to think of it in relation to the neighbouring plants rather than in isolation. It is not easy to envisage the finished scene, but try to get a general impression in your mind's eye before starting to plant.

Sunflowers thrive in a sunny position (preferably south-facing), and love well-drained, deep soil. However, unlike many other plants, they grow well

Sunflowers are beautiful *and* useful.

almost anywhere, so it is easy to find a variety to suit most uses.

Sunflowers are ideal for growing in containers, so you can grow them, whatever the size of your garden, patio or balcony (see box on page 17). Make sure that your container has good drainage, and that you use compost, not soil from the garden, which may harbour pests and diseases.

Sunflowers come in a range of heights and a wide spectrum of colors within the golden-yellow to red-brown palette. Some varieties can be used as edging plants, while others will give height to the back of a border. They also make wonderful focal points and will disguise or distract from an eyesore.

If you plan to grow sunflowers as a crop, do not feel you have to banish them to the vegetable patch. Just plant them among the flowers in the border. They will look wonderful wherever they are.

Consider the ultimate height of whichever variety you choose – anything too tall will look silly edging a path and may obscure the plants behind. Similarly, you do not want to lose a shorter variety among the general hubbub of the border.

Consider colors carefully at the planning stage and you will avoid disastrous clashes later. Keeping the combinations simple is the surest way to ensure success. Sunflowers come in numerous sun shades, from muted, reddish-brown autumnal hues, such as 'Evening Sun', to the hot, Mediterranean yellow of 'Sunspot', so there is no lack of choice. Yellow-orangey shades are very close to green on the color spectrum, which means they look good with most foliage – especially silvery-grey and light green. Yellow is also, like white, a very luminous, 'advancing' color, which means it is useful to brighten up drab areas of the garden, and will look spectacular in the

There are sunflowers
of all shapes and sizes
to suit every garden.

evening as dusk starts to fall.

A single, tall sunflower can make an extremely dramatic statement, especially in a small garden or in a pot on the terrace. However, if you are planting shorter varieties in a large garden, their effectiveness may be dissipated if they are dotted about. To look their best it is worth planting in large groups.

Once you've got a basic idea of what you are aiming for, sit down and draw up a simple plan of where you want your plants to go. This is not difficult or time-consuming and is a good way of getting plant requirements, sizes, heights and flowering times firmly fixed in your mind.

PREPARATION

Once all this is done it is time to prepare the soil for planting. Luckily, sunflowers are wonderfully unfussy and, unless you are growing giant sunflowers (see pages 22-3), will be quite content on rich or poor soil – as long as it is well-drained and in a sunny position.

So there is no need to use vast quantities of compost. They do like a bit of space, however, so will be happiest in a deep bed, well forked over.

If you are planting young, bought perennials, they should go into the ground in mid- to late autumn or mid-spring. However, if you are sowing seeds, the optimum time is early to mid-spring.

If you have the space and time, you can sow seeds in individual pots and place them on a warm windowsill, or in a propagator to encourage them to germinate before moving into the garden. However, unless you are growing giant sunflowers this isn't necessary, and they will do perfectly well sown directly into their permanent position. In fact, this may encourage them to grow a stronger root system.

Sow your seeds approximately 1 in/2.5 cm deep, at a distance of 1 1/2-2 ft/45-60 cm. Remember, many little animals and birds find seedlings very tasty, so you may need netting to keep away hungry pests (see Caring for Sunflowers, pages 24-5).

Which variety?

The variety of sunflower you choose to grow will depend on what you want from your sunflowers. For example, are you looking for flowers for cutting, or to provide a decorative focal point in the garden, or do you want to grow a giant sunflower to break records? Or maybe you are simply interested in a crop. Whatever your requirements, there is a variety to suit you.

The sunflower family is divided into two basic groups: annuals and perennials. The sunflower most people tend to picture is the annual, *Helianthus annuus*. Yet there are also numerous varieties of perennials which look different, tending to be smaller, and bushier than the familiar single, yellow bloom. And there are single and double varieties of both!

AS A FOCAL POINT

The taller varieties make natural focal points, attracting the eye with their architectural elegance and sheer extravagance of size. The ultimate focal point must surely be a giant sunflower (see pages 22-3). Some varieties can grow to 15 ft/4.5 m tall!

Yellow will naturally attract the human eye because we recognize yellow faster than any other color; however, the more unusually colored sunflowers also make splendid focal points. The mere fact that they are not the yellow everyone expects sunflowers to be is enough to make people look twice. For example, 'Velvet Queen' (5-6 ft/1.5-1.8 m), has rich, baroque coloring; a black centre framed by blood-red petals – guaranteed to be a talking point. A total contrast colorwise is 'Italian White' (4-6 ft/1.2-1.8 m). Its flowerheads are also black centerd, yet they are surrounded by crisp, creamy white petals.

AS A CROP

Most of the crop-producing sunflowers are yellow. Go for the varieties that promise large heads because they produce the largest seeds. One of the best varieties is 'Peredovik' (height 5-6 ft/1.5-1.8 m, head size 4-6

in/10-15 cm). The shells on the seeds are very thin, which means they can be removed by hand, making this variety an excellent choice for the gardener. Other good varieties are 'Jumbo' (height 8 ft/2.4 m, head size 1 ft/30 cm), and the giant varieties, such as 'Paul Bunyon' (height 15 ft/4.5 m, head size 20 in/50 cm).

FOR CUTTING

The enormous range of colors and sizes are an inspiration to any flower arranger. Among the many varieties worth looking for are 'Sonja' (3 ft/90 cm) with strong orange flowers, 10 cm/4 in across, with rich brown centers, and any variety with double flowers, such as the golden-yellow 'Loddon Gold' (5 ft/1.5 m). The varieties with different color combinations are excellent for cutting, as well as looking very pretty in the garden. 'Color Fashion Mix' (6 ft/1.8 m) comes in reds and purples, besides the more usual yellows.

TO DELIGHT CHILDREN

You could grow one of the giant varieties, but I think children will have more fun with sunflowers closer to their own height. They have the advantage of being manageable, while still giving that *Alice In Wonderland* feel. For little children, 'Sunspot' is ideal. It only grows a couple of feet tall, yet produces a flower 8-10 in/20-25 cm in diameter. Older children will love 'Holiday' (4-5 ft/1.2-1.5 m) and 'Southern Lights', which grows to the same height and is available in a mixture of beautiful colors, from gold, to deep reds and browns.

Why not try planting a living playhouse, by planting sunflowers in a circle? Remember to leave a gap for an entrance! (See photograph on page 67.)

FOR BORDERS

For edging a border, the shorter varieties come into their own, such as 'Sonja' (3 ft/90 cm), which has orange flowers with rich brown centres, and 'Teddy Bear' (1-2 ft/40-60 cm). 'Taiyo' (4-10 ft/1.2-3 m), is very pretty, with yellow petals surrounding a dark seedhead. Further back in the border, the bushier perennials such as *Helianthus* x *multiflorus* (5 ft/1.5 m) look wonderful, as does the dramatically-named 'Saw-tooth Sunflower' (2-8 ft/60 cm-2.4 m).

Not all sunflowers are yellow! 'Italian White' (far left) and 'Velvet Queen' (center).

The fluffy, rich yellow 'Teddy Bear' (left) appeals to adults and children alike.

Growing in containers

Don't be turned off by the great heights that some sunflowers can grow to. They can thrive in containers and make striking and unusual subjects, for gardens or patios of all sizes. Sunflowers will not flourish if cramped, so a deep, large container is essential. A tub or half barrel is ideal, and works particularly well for a simple, informal arrangement.

Garden design schemes

As long as the most basic requirements of sunflowers are satisfied (a sunny location, some support and well-drained soil), they will bloom just as happily in a container on a little town terrace as in a huge border of a country garden – so anything goes!

A GARDEN KITCHEN

Sunflowers look especially good in terracotta pots; these make natural partners, possibly because they are both associated with the Mediterranean. A deep, terracotta pot planted with sunflowers, surrounded by a selection of herbs (for example bay, fennel, rosemary and French tarragon), makes a fragrant and practical display for outside a kitchen window.

PLANTS IN POTS

A collection of large, plain, deep flowerpots planted with sunflowers, makes an unusual informal screen and has the advantage of being moveable. One day they could be placed side-by-side separating an outside eating area or terrace from the rest of the garden, while the next, they could be lined up like a guard of honor alongside a path. They also look very dramatic arranged in a semi-circle behind a sunny, south-facing seat.

If placed near a window, a container filled with sunflowers can also be very entertaining, because sunflower seeds are irresistible to a wide variety of birds. It is much more fun, and attractive, to have a living bird feeder than a conventional one. A word of warning, however: sunflowers also attract a lot of insects, particularly bees, so do not put the container too close to any window that you tend to leave open.

COTTAGE GARDEN

Cottage gardens, with their tumbling abundance of plants, colors and perfumes, evoke the spirit of Olde England. The cottage garden look is one of controlled confusion, with beds containing a mixture of flowers, fruit and vegetables. This heady style came about from necessity rather than design. Cottage dwellers had little land and needed to grow fruit and vegetables for food, yet they also wanted to grow flowers and so, space being tight, they chose flowers which would look spectacular and could rise above their humble bedfellows. Sunflowers, which fulfill that role to perfection, are as much a part of cottage gardens as hollyhocks and old shrub roses.

To re-create this look, plant your sunflowers at the back of the border or in rows with other cottage garden favorites – such as *Solidago* (golden rod), rudbeckias, globe thistles (*Echinops*) and hollyhocks. Basically, plan your border with the tallest at the back, and shortest at the front. Remember to leave room at the front for your vegetable and herb crops.

If you have a very straight path leading to a door or gate, line it with fragrant lavender and arrange your sunflowers at the end to frame the opening. Being so tall, the sunflowers look wonderfully inviting, and the combination of blue and yellow is irresistible. Choose any of the traditional yellow sunflowers because they would have been the only ones available.

NEW ENGLAND

Early Fall in New England is characterized by roadside stalls piled high with colorful squash and ornamental gourds, and fields full of ripening corn. This is also when sunflowers come into their own, livening up gardens when the colorful, herbaceous plants of summer start to die back. Sunflowers are a significant part of the North American landscape (in fact, many Americans are lobbying for sunflowers to be adopted as the national flower), pairing them with squashes or corn seems a natural combination.

Corn and sunflowers planted together become mutually protective, shielding one another from the worst of any high winds. Not surprisingly, if grown together, the yield of each will increase. Grown with squash, the sunflowers act as valuable supports, providing growing canes for the plants to trail up. The richly colored squash also look very pretty beside the tall, bright-faced sunflowers.

ARCHITECTURAL

There are plants and flowers which are almost pieces of sculpture in their own right. Such plants add a wonderful, architectural element to a garden, providing a counterpoint to the fluffier and often floppier, herbaceous plants. Sunflowers, having immense stature and elegance, are just such plants

Sunflowers thrive in pots (above).
To create an authentic cottage garden,
sunflowers are essential (left).

and when grown with other plants with similar qualities will transform the most mundane garden into something truly spectacular.

You will have your own favorites, but why not experiment with stately agapanthus and magnificent euphorbias and alliums. Another perfect companion (having exactly the same light and soil requirements), is globe thistle (*Echinops*). *Echinops sphaerocephalus* can grow to 2 m/6 ft, and has dramatic, almost alien-looking, grey-white flower heads.

Combine these tall stars with fennel, with its delicate, decorative, feathery foliage. Bronze fennel (*Foeniculum vulgare* 'Purpureum'), will look especially glorious, or rodgersia, which has fluffy creamy-white flowers. These will look particularly theatrical with one of the darker sunflowers, such as 'Prado Red'.

COPING WITH LIGHT AND SHADE

Most gardens have a corner in which bright sunshine and shade exist side-by-side, often where a wall or building casts a shadow. It can sometimes be difficult to find plants that will look good beside one another, yet be happy with these different conditions.

To make the most of your sunflowers, you need to plant them in sunlight, near a wall, so you need to find companion plants that will thrive in the shade cast by the wall and the sunflowers.

One approach is to go for the attraction of opposites. Sunflowers and hostas could not be more different, yet they go amazingly well together. The low-lying hostas make the sunflowers look especially tall and bright, while the hostas, in their turn, look even more sophisticated than usual when contrasted with the golden blooms of their upright, cheerful neighbors. Hostas with very broad leaves, such as *Hosta sieboldiana* 'Frances Williams' and *Hosta crispula* work best. Choose medium-sized varieties of sunflowers, such as 'Sungold Double' and 'Prado Yellow'. The only drawback with this scheme is that it will prove extremely popular with slugs, so some protection is vital (see page 25).

Garden color schemes

Most gardeners learn through trial and error that there is a skill to combining colors. Some work wonderfully together, while others either look too garish or become wishy-washy. For example, pale yellow-orange flowers will suddenly seem less intense if planted beside clear yellow flowers. Here are some color scheming ideas that work with yellow sunflowers, being the most widely available. For color co-ordinating with the more unusually-colored sunflowers, use the color wheel for guidance (below right). Remember that warm and cool colors have different characteristics – warm colors are stimulating and advancing, so have a foreshortening effect, while cool colors are calming and receding, creating a greater feeling of distance.

YELLOW AND GREEN

Yellow and green make a classic combination, which never fails to work wonderfully. For something really different, seek out some calming green flowers to plant in front of your busy, bright sunflowers. Green flowers always cause a stir, being slightly disconcerting, while remaining extremely attractive.

Use *Nicotiana alata* 'Lime Green', with its pretty little trumpet-shaped flowers, and *Moluccella* (Bells of Ireland, also known as shell flowers), which has spikes of tiny, tubular, white flowers surrounded by a pale green calyx. Variegated evergreen shrubs, such as golden privet (*Ligustrum ovalifolium* 'Aureum'), and *Euonymus fortunei* 'Emerald 'n' Gold', will also work well in this scheme, providing structure and contrast.

YELLOW AND BLUE

Blue and yellow look very pretty together, and there is such a tremendous variety of beautiful blue flowers to choose from, that no-one could fail to be inspired.

For a border scheme that is graceful, yet grand enough for an English country house, choose a perennial sunflower such as 'Loddon Gold', and team it up with elegant delphiniums. Add some *Echinops ritro* or lofty *Echinops bannaticus* and *Campanula lactiflora* – 'Prichard's Variety' is lovely. Continuing the aristocratic theme, add some agapanthus (with their tall globes of blue flower), and some Michaelmas daisies. And don't forget lavender, which is an ideal edging plant for a border, and also smells wonderful on a summer evening.

You can create a color scheme in the smallest of spaces (left).

'Jewel of Africa' nasturtiums look beautiful planted with sunflowers and also deter aphids (top right).

Sunflowers add a welcome splash of color to any garden scene (above right).

YELLOW AND WHITE

This combination is tremendously luminous, and will almost seem to glow on a warm, summer's evening. Bearing in mind how particularly attractive these colors look at dusk, choose some flowers which release their fragrance at this time to create a deliciously sensuous scene.

For beautiful, highly-scented flowers, lilies and nicotiana (flowering tobacco plants) cannot be surpassed. There are numerous lilies, both white and yellow, which would be ideal. It is worth looking out for the tall *Lilium auratum* (golden-rayed lily of Japan), or *Lilium wallichianum*. While among the tobacco plants, *Nicotiana alata* or *N. sylvestris*, are obvious candidates. For a really dazzling display, plant some *Phlox paniculata* 'Snow Queen', with the starkly vertical *Lysimachia ephereum* (loosestrife) and some *Aster tradescantii* to hide all the tall stems.

YELLOW AND ORANGE

Yellow and orange are a fiery combination, yet being neighbors on the color wheel they harmonize perfectly. Start by planting two or three varieties of golden-orange and yellow sunflowers. There are plenty to choose from, such as 'Oranges and Lemons', 'Sungold Double' or 'Sunbeam'. Then surround them with a sunny sea of solidago, helenium (sneezeweed), yellow loosestrife (*Lysimachia punctata*), rudbeckia, heliopsis and *Alchemilla mollis*. The shorter tagetes and calendula (marigold), make a colorful, bushy edging. Try to keep different shades in blocks so that the colors are not diluted.

Yellow and green   **Yellow and orange**

Choose neighboring colors on the color wheel for an harmonious, subtle scheme.

Yellow and white   **Yellow and blue**

For a more dramatic scheme, opt for colors on opposite sides of the wheel.

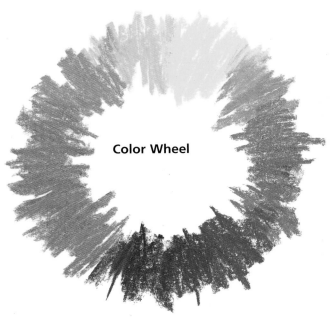

Color Wheel

Growing giant sunflowers

There is nothing like a giant sunflower to bring out the child in us all. They have the ability to capture the imagination of even the most jaded adult and can make the tallest man feel like Gulliver. Every seed that is planted is accompanied by a feeling of excitement and anticipation, and the hope that this may be the one to break the record! At the very least, you should be able to grow a sunflower 12-15 ft/3.6-4.5 m tall.

VARIETIES

Do not think that any sunflower given the right treatment will grow huge. Only certain varieties contain the genetic properties to become enormous. The ones to grow are 'Russian Giant', 'Mammoth Grey Stripe' (also known as 'Giant Grey Stripe' and 'Mammoth Russian') or 'Paul Bunyon', although many garden centers sell seeds simply labeled 'giant'.

SITE AND PLANTING

Like other varieties of sunflower, giants like a south-facing site on well-drained, deep soil, preferably against a wall for protection. However, if you are aiming for height rather than flower size, then plant against a north-facing wall. The thinking behind this is that the sunflower will grow tall trying to reach the morning sun. Avoid very high walls as they would leave the plant too much in the dark, and do not plant too close to the wall – a 8 ft/2.4 m gap is ideal.

Even those with a tiny garden or nothing bigger than a balcony can have a go, as it is still possible to grow giants in large containers or raised beds.

The best time to sow is early spring. There are two methods, each with their own pros and cons. The first method is to sow directly into the ground. This has the advantage of being simple and quick, yet you have less control over the results. The second method, using a propagator, is much more time-consuming, but cuts down on the element of chance – for example a late cold snap or high winds. You can also reject any puny seedlings right from the start.

SOWING DIRECT

Make a series of holes, about 1 in/ 2.5 cm deep and 3 ft/1 m apart and plant about three seeds in each hole. Once the seeds have germinated, thin out, leaving only the strongest one from each batch. Stake each plant to a cane and protect with a windbreak (fine plastic mesh is ideal).

USING A PROPAGATOR

Sow the seeds in small compost-filled pots, one seed per pot, ensuring the compost is thoroughly damp. Place the pots in a covered propagator to germinate, which should take approximately 7-10 days. Once the leaves start to appear, keep a sharp look out for any signs of fungus, which thrive in these warm, humid conditions. Spray with fungicide if necessary. Once the plant has four leaves or more it is ready to be planted outside. Space, stake and protect from wind as with sowing direct.

AFTERCARE

It is important to ensure that your young sunflowers are well supported. As they get going they will grow very fast, so you will need to check their ties regularly and replace their initial canes with sturdier stakes as they become taller and heavier. Heaping up a mound of earth around the base of the stem will add stability.

Giant sunflowers need regular feeding and watering. Get into a routine of keeping your plants well watered, especially during any prolonged dry spells, as this will benefit your plant far more than an occasional massive soak. A weekly feed of liquid seaweed or an all-purpose liquid or soluble fertilizer is sufficient for the main growing period, although to get really spectacular results, change the feeding routine once the sunflower is mature enough to start developing a flower. A liquid fertilizer with a high potash formula will work wonders in encouraging the flower head to develop well.

Be constantly vigilant for any sign of attack from pests or disease. Prevention is always better than cure, so follow the precautions on pages 24-5.

Record breaker Bernard Lavery with his giant sunflowers (above left).

'Giant Yellow' can grow to 9 ft/2.7 m (above right).

If you want to grow large flower heads, opt for 'F1 Full Sun' (below).

Record Breakers

A sunflower grown by M Heijms, Oirschot, Netherlands in 1986 was recorded at 25 ft 5½ in/7.76 m tall.

A sunflower with a head of 32¼ in/82 cm in diameter was grown by Emily Martin of Maple Ridge, British Columbia, Canada in September 1983.

Caring for sunflowers

Sunflowers demand remarkably little special treatment. Unless you are growing giant sunflowers (see pages 22-3) you will find that, apart from fending off pests and disease, you can reap great rewards with very little effort.

GENERAL CARE

Sunflowers do not require constant feeding – in fact, hungry sunflowers produce more blooms – and they will also grow well in any ordinary, well-drained garden soil. Similarly, they do not need the never-ending watering demanded by other plants; overwatering only serves to inhibit flower growth, although a thick dressing of mulch will help to preserve moisture in dry periods. It is important, however, to give them a good start by digging in compost or a general purpose fertiliser when planting.

The very tall varieties will need some support if they are exposed to strong winds. Tie them to vine eyes if they are against a wall or fence, or use stakes elsewhere in the garden. Generally they will happily support themselves and even act as living canes for smaller plants to scramble up.

After the perennial sunflowers have finished their wonderful floral display, they should, like other herbaceous plants, be deadheaded, then later be cut back to the ground. In addition, any double varieties of perennials should be divided every third or fourth year to discourage them from becoming single again.

PROPAGATION

Perennial sunflowers can be propagated by division. This is a wonderfully cheap and easy way of increasing stock, and is very good for the health and vigour of your plants because you discard any old dead material. Like all herbaceous perennials, sunflowers have a dormant period after they have died back (between late autumn and mid spring).

This is the time to divide them up as they will put up with a great deal of root disturbance.

Dividing young plants is simple. Using a garden fork, loosen the soil until you are able to lever up the roots, which will look like matted clumps. Shake off any excess soil. To remove particularly obstinate soil, submerge the whole mass in a bucket filled with tepid water. Next, carefully pull the knotted root mass apart by hand or with a small hand fork. You want to divide the root so each clump has five or six shoots. Take a sharp knife and trim off any dead roots and foliage. Re-plant immediately making sure you firm down the soil and water the sites thoroughly. If you are left with any very small clumps, it is best to pot them up or put them in a nursery bed until they become a bit bigger and stronger – they should be ready for their permanent position by the following autumn.

Mature plants can be much tougher to divide, and if the clump has an especially woody centre, you may need to chop through it with a spade. Once you've succeeded, cut away any dead woody material before replanting.

PESTS AND DISEASES

Sunflowers are very hardy, but like all plants suffer their fair share of disease and attack by pests. Prevention is always better than cure, and many diseases can be thwarted by good husbandry, such as choosing an appropriate site, careful preparation, planting and ongoing attention. As far as pests are concerned, thorough netting is the key, after that,

Two eco-friendly and cost-effective ways of deterring aphids: spraying with soapy water (right), and companion planting with chives (far right).

constant vigilance is vital.

To ensure a beautiful display and a healthy, productive crop, keep a watchful eye open for the following pests and diseases:

GREY MOLD

This unpleasant condition is caused by a fungus called *Botrytis cinerea*. It appears as a soft, smoky whitish-grey mold which can rot any part of the plant. It is particularly active in wet weather and does not restrict itself to young plants, but will attack established ones as well before spreading to adjacent plants if left unchecked. The cure is to destroy all affected material (by burning, not by putting on the compost heap), and spray with a fungicide. However there is also a prevention. As the fungus tends to attack soft growth, a liberal sprinkling of potash on the ground before planting will harden up growth and so deter attack.

POWDERY MILDEW

It is easy to recognize an attack by this fungus as a whitish powdery growth will appear on the upper surface of the leaves. If left untreated it will soon spread to the rest of the plant, then from there, through rain splash and wind, to its neighbours so prompt action is vital. As with grey mold, remove and destroy affected growth then spray with a suitable fungicide. If you have regular trouble with this disease, avoid grouping the plants too densely, and check that the soil is not too dry.

SLUGS AND SNAILS

Slugs are especially keen on soft leaves and stems, and emerge from their hiding places at night to do a great deal of damage before vanishing again. The first thing to do is to tidy up piles of leaves, weeds and any other garden debris, which could shelter them, and avoid using excessive amounts of organic matter, which could attract them. They cannot abide gritty, spiky material, so sprinkle gravel, old ashes or holly leaves around the base of your flowers. You could also set traps of orange and grapefruit peel or even submerge a jam jar full of beer in the ground up to its rim, to ensure a wet, but happy, death. As a last resort there is poisoned bait, such as slug pellets. However, avoid these if at all possible, as they are very dangerous to children, animals and birds.

APHIDS

Aphids are particularly fond of sunflowers, so check the flower heads regularly for any sign of them. Companion planting can be very effective for discouraging aphids. For example, chives or nasturtiums will both deter aphids. Aphids cannot abide the smell of chives, while nasturtiums (*Tropaeolum*), work in a different way, attracting the aphids away from the sunflowers with the promise of a tasty feast. You could also spray your sunflowers daily with soapy water or, as a last resort, use a systemic insecticide.

MICE AND RABBITS

The only way to keep rabbits away is to erect a chicken wire fence around the flowers. This must go a few feet underground to prevent the rabbits burrowing underneath. Bend the buried wire outwards for best effect. Mice can also be troublesome pests, particularly early in the season, so lay traps or bait at the first sign of them... or, as a last resort, buy a cat.

BIRDS

The fact that some sunflowers (notably 'Peredovik'), are grown for bird food gives some clue as to how much birds adore the seeds. Bird scarers can be very effective, but the noisier ones will not make you popular with the neighbours, in which case, netting works well. Choose net with holes just big enough to allow access to pollinating insects. But the fact that sunflowers are so attractive to birds is not totally disastrous, because before eating your seeds, they will eat any insects lurking on your plants.

Sunflower

craft

If you adore sunflowers growing in the garden and arranged in vases, then go one step further and adopt the cheerful sunflower as your personal logo. To create an atmosphere positively buzzing with optimism, bring sunflowers into every area of your home and life. Brighten up your kitchen or child's bedroom with a gay sunflower frieze, create a unique picture frame, decorated with seeds, and dine by candlelight – courtesy of a sunflower candleholder – at a table adorned with a sunflower pot-et-fleurs. You could also individualise your most precious books with sunflower stamps, and make beautiful cards, bookmarks and frames to give as gifts.

Preserving sunflowers

Sunflowers look glorious freshly cut, but why discard all that beauty once their season has finished? Instead, preserve them and capture a bit of summer to cheer up gloomy winter days. You can arrange dried sunflowers with other dried and fresh flowers (see page 46), or use dried seeds and petals in numerous craft projects.

Remember that sunflowers offer more than just a pretty face. They are also a valuable crop, grown across the world for their nutritious and delicious seeds and the oil that can be made from these. So, while drying flowers to decorate your home, put some sunflower seeds aside to dry for use in your cooking.

DRYING WHOLE SUNFLOWERS

Sunflowers are suitable for drying once they have reached their open stage, but before they become too 'ripe'. A simple way to tell what stage they are at is to check the seedhead. If you can see pollen then the sunflowers have passed their best.

Pick the flowers on a dry day, early in the morning. Do not pick them too early, before the dew has evaporated. You will need a dry, dark place with good air circulation to dry the flowers such as an attic or garage. To avoid rot there should be good air flow. Avoid direct sunlight which might discolor the flowers. Some fading of the color must be expected, however the faster the flowers dry, the brighter the final color will be. You can also dry sunflowers that you have bought. Do not wait for the sunflowers to be past their best before drying them. You can admire them fresh for 2-3 days, and then dry them.

There are two methods of drying suitable for sunflowers: flat drying and air drying. Both are wonderfully straightforward.

FLAT DRYING

If your sunflowers have very large seedheads, it is better to dry them flat. They can be laid on paper on the floor, although make sure the floor is spotlessly clean and totally dry. But by far the best method is to dry them on slatted, wooden shelves, on absorbent paper – paper towels are ideal. Position the heads so that they do not touch, then trim off all but a stub of stem (needed for wiring), and push this down through the paper. The flowerhead will now be facing the ceiling. Keep a check on the paper and renew if damp.

Alternatively, you could make your own drying frame. Simply take four equal-sized pieces of wood, nail at right angles to form a frame, then cover with chicken wire.

AIR DRYING

This is the easiest method. Simply secure a small bunch of sunflowers with an elastic band and hang upside-down, leaving ample space between the bunches to ensure good air circulation. Leave for at least three weeks or until you are sure the whole stem has dried out. Feel the point where the stem meets the flowerhead to test if it is ready, as this will be the last part to dry.

WIRING SUNFLOWERS

It is vital to master this very basic skill if you are planning to arrange dried sunflowers, or indeed, any other flowers. Besides lengthening or reinforcing a short stem, wire can be used to create a completely false stem or to secure a few flowers into a bunch.

If you have dried your sunflower flat you will only have a stub of stem left to work with. Obviously this is too short for any arrangement, so extend it by binding the stem to a thin cane using gutta-percha tape (a stretchy, rubber-based tape that comes in green and brown), or with stub (floral) wire.

If you need to make a bunch of dried sunflowers, cut all the stems to the same length then wrap the stub wire four or five times around the middle of the stem making sure it is tight enough to hold the stems firmly, while not so tight as to damage them.

DRYING SUNFLOWER SEEDS

Sunflower seeds are extremely useful, and they are very easy to dry. You should expect a fully-grown sunflower to yield anything between 250-1,500 seeds, with the largest coming from the rings of seeds on the outermost edge of the head.

Examine your sunflowers carefully before deciding which sunflowers to reserve for seeds. The largest heads will produce the most seeds, and these are the ones you need. Don't cut these until the petals

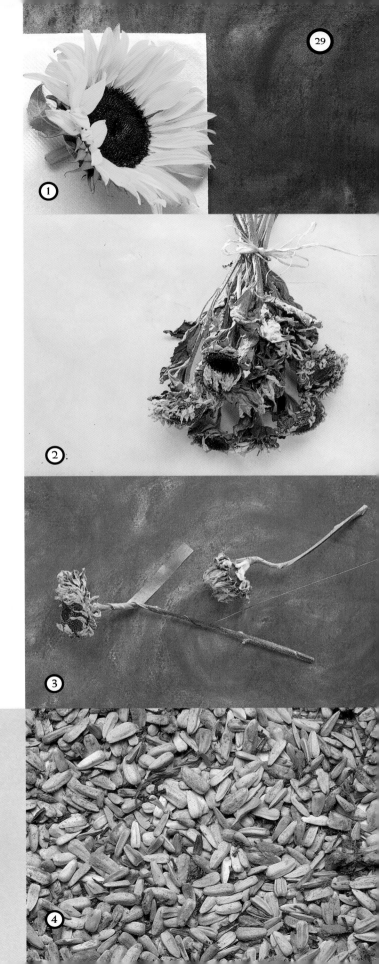

have dried. You will also see that the stamen will drop off and the back of the flowerhead will turn brown.

Always inspect the seeds themselves – they should look plump and ripe. But the surest sign that your crop is ripe, is the appearance of flocks of birds. Be sure not to let them get the chance to harvest your sunflower seeds for themselves!

Harvesting the seeds is not difficult. First, cut off the seedhead, then bend the sides of the head back and use a spoon to lever the seeds out. Alternatively, pick the seeds out with your fingers. Smaller seeds can be removed with a stiff brush, or the heads can be rubbed against rough hessian mounted on a wooden frame. Use a bucket or box to catch the seeds as they fall. It is important to remove the seeds from the flowers as soon as possible after harvesting, before mold can get established.

To dry the seeds, spread them out in a shallow basket or wooden tray and leave them somewhere warm, such as an airing cupboard to dry out. As with drying flowers, good air circulation is vital. They should be dry in 3-4 weeks.

When the seeds are dry you will need to remove the husks. These can be removed by hand, although it is a time-consuming, awkward job, so if you plan to harvest a large number of seeds, it will be worthwhile buying a machine to do the job for you. However, if you are planning to store the seeds, leave their shells on as they will stay fresher for longer.

Seeds for planting will keep perfectly well for a couple of years if stored in an airtight container in a cool, dry place. However, if you are planning to use them as an ingredient, only keep them for a few months. This is because their natural polyunsaturated oils will turn rancid. The seed's color will tell you if it is fresh or not: good seeds are pale grey, while bad ones turn yellowy-brown.

① **Flat drying**

② **Air drying**

③ **Wiring sunflowers**

④ **Dried sunflower seeds**

Pressing petals and flowers

There is something quite magical about pressing petals and flowers. It enables one to preserve something so fragile and normally short-lived, as though the normal cycle of death and renewal is somehow suspended and a moment in time captured and preserved forever.

Some of the small varieties of sunflower press very well, but for the most part, you will get better results from pressing sunflower petals. The problem with pressing most sunflowers is that the central disc is often bulky and can prevent the petals from drying absolutely flat. Sunflower petals are an immensely suitable and satisfying subject for pressing as they are large and therefore easy to work with. Another advantage of drying and pressing the petals separately, is that while air drying tends to produce rather brown, shrivelled petals, pressing preserves their shape and captures the bright, sunny colors so much a part of the sunflower's character. The secret is speed; the faster the petals dry in the press, the brighter the colors will be.

Colors do alter slightly when dried. Yellow, orange and red become darker (yet somehow richer), while white petals turn a creamy, parchment color. Be sure to grow different varieties to provide a selection of sunflower colors, or plant a good mixed variety – such as 'Color Fashion Mix', 'Discovery Mix' or 'Inca Jewels'.

CHOOSING AND GATHERING

Only select perfect flowers and petals to press, and collect them soon after they have bloomed when their color will be at its best. Material must be dry when picked, so avoid the early part of the day when there may still be traces of dew.

Once picked, or bought, press as soon as possible to preserve the color and freshness.

There are numerous excellent and inexpensive flower presses available, although the cheapest and simplest method is to use a big, thick book!

MATERIALS
❀ few sheets of absorbent paper, such as blotting paper or paper towels ❀ big, thick book

METHOD
1 Place the petals or flowers you plan to press on a sheet of absorbent paper in the center of the book.
2 Put another sheet of absorbent paper on top, then gently roll the pages shut.
3 Leave the book in a dry, airy place (such as an airing cupboard), with a weight on top if you wish, for a couple weeks.
4 Check once for mildew, otherwise do not disturb.

SEEDS FOR CRAFT WORK
One of the joys of sunflowers is the enormous number of varieties now available in so many different colors. This wide range of colors is not confined to the petals; the central discs also come in a numerous striking hues, ranging from green to rich red. Certain varieties are valued, especially for their decorative seeds; in fact, these can be so attractive that they are worth saving as a decorative feature. The seeds from the giant varieties are the easiest to work with, being less awkward.

Among the varieties with particularly unusual seeds are:

'Mammoth Russian'
(a.k.a. Mammoth Grey Stripe):
broad, thin-shelled, grey and white striped seeds
'Hopi Dye':
thin-shelled, purple-black seeds
'Jumbo':
large black and white striped seeds
'Peredovik':
pure black elongated seeds
'Israeli':
large black and white seeds
'Tarahumara White Shelled':
unsurprisingly, white-shelled seeds
'Sundak':
large seeds, with grey and black stripes

STENCILS AND STAMPS

There are a wide range of stencils and rubber stamps available with very pretty sunflower designs. They can be used in many ways – from decorating pots to decorating a whole room. They are also ideal for decorating writing paper, greetings cards, T-shirts, party invitations... the list is endless. You could also try making your own stamps and stencils.

Making a stencil

MATERIALS

❀ sunflower design ❀ masking tape ❀ couple of sheets of thick acetate ❀ fine felt-tip marker pen ❀ cutting mat ❀ sharp craft knife

METHOD

1 Place your sunflower design on a flat surface and secure with masking tape to prevent it slipping.

2 Position the acetate on top of it and similarly secure, then trace the outline of the sunflower petals using the felt-tip marker.

3 Next place a new piece of acetate on top of the sunflower picture and trace the central disc.

4 Transfer the first piece of acetate on to the cutting mat and again fix with masking tape, then carefully cut out the petal outline using the craft knife. Leave a border a good 2 in/5 cm deep to allow for overlapping brush strokes.

5 Secure the second piece of acetate on the cutting mat and cut out the central disc.

6 When you are ready to paint you may find it easier to stencil the central disc first then, when it has dried, stencil the petals around it.

Flower cushion

Sunflowers are the inspiration for hundreds of beautiful fabrics, soft furnishings, needlepoint and knitwear designs. Why not take some of the sunflower images in this book as the starting point for your own unique design.

Sunflower design by Kaffe Fassett (left).

Sunflower candle

A single, giant sunflower can make an unusual candle holder. The warm light of the candle will give you the opportunity to examine, and appreciate, the complex and beautiful seed pattern of the sunflower. Also, the way that sunflower petals dry make it look as though they are reaching up towards the flame.

MATERIALS

❀ large sunflower head ❀ florist's foam (oasis) ❀ shallow bowl ❀ sharp knife ❀ floral adhesive tape ❀ spiked, metal-lined, plastic candleholder (these can be bought ready-made) ❀ candle

METHOD

1 Remove the stem from the sunflower head.

2 Using a sharp knife, cut a piece of florist's foam to fit the bowl. Then cut a circle in the centre of the seedhead, just wide enough to take the candleholder.

3 Place the flowerhead flat on top of the foam, using a few loops of floral adhesive tape to secure it. Insert the candleholder through the hole, and press firmly into the foam, making sure the top of the candle holder lies below the surface of the seedhead, so it is not visible.

4 Add a candle of your choice, and light. A thin cream candle will look very stylish, or you could use a contrasting color for a more up-tempo feel.

Greetings cards and bookmarks

MATERIALS

✿ thick card (dark colors, such as deep blue, rich green or black are best, as pale colors can look wishy-washy) ✿ scissors ✿ plain paper ✿ colored pencils ✿ glue pen ✿ pressed petals ✿ tweezers ✿ hair spray

METHOD

1 To make a greetings card, take a rectangular piece of card and fold in half lengthways, then run the outside edge of a pair if scissors along the fold to make it flat. If you are making a bookmark, simply cut the card into the shape you require.

2 Cut a piece of plain paper to the same size, and using the colored pencils, work out a rough design. This stage is especially important for beginners as the dried, pressed petals are very delicate and if you have a rough design to follow you can avoid over-handling them. As you get more skilled you can make up a design as you go along.

3 Dot the glue where needed, then gently lift the petals with the tweezers and place where required.

4 When the design is complete, fix the petals with a light film of hair spray.

Photograph frames

There are numerous cheap, plain photograph frames in the shops, all crying out to be transformed into something totally unique and special. This method can be scaled up for mirrors or picture frames.

MATERIALS

✿ plain paper ✿ colored pencils ✿ glue pen ✿ plain photograph frame ✿ pressed petals ✿ tweezers ✿ hair spray

METHOD

1 Using the plain paper and colored pencils, rough up a design, keeping it as simple as possible to get the best effect.

2 Spread glue on the frame, before positioning the petals with the tweezers, according to your plan.

3 Fix with a thin film of hair spray.

Terracotta pot

Transform a terracotta pot by creating a decorative band around its rim with pretty seeds. Keep the design simple – it will be especially striking if you use seeds with strong contrasting colors, such as black seeds with white or pale grey seeds. One variety may be sufficient if the seeds are particularly striking.

MATERIALS

✿ tape measure ✿ terracotta flowerpot (available at any good garden center) ✿ graph paper ✿ dried seeds ✿ glue ✿ tweezers ✿ hair spray

METHOD

1 Measure the circumference of the pot, then take a sheet of graph paper and sketch out a rough design to the same scale.

2 Arrange the seeds, according to your design, on the paper.

3 Spread the glue on the pot and carefully – referring to your design – stick on the seeds, using tweezers, in the order they are arranged in front of you.

4 Finally, fix with a thin film of hair spray.

Pot-et-fleurs

MATERIALS

✿ florist's foam (oasis) ✿ small terracotta or china pot ✿ thick candle ✿ a selection of small sunflowers (fresh or dried), wired

METHOD

1 Cut a piece of florist's foam to fit the pot. You can push the pot onto the florist's foam to get the rough size and shape.

2 Hollow out a hole in the middle for the candle, and add the candle.

3 Arrange the sunflowers around the edge of the pot, bending the wire to tilt their heads outwards.

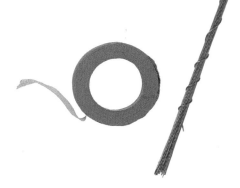

Flower arranging with sunflowers

A few decades ago it would have been considered quite eccentric to have sunflowers inside the home – they were classed as a crop, whose place was in the field, kitchen or cottage garden. Now there is no bar to using these gloriously bright and cheerful flowers to bring the beauty of summer into the home. And, with careful drying, we can have sunflowers in the home, all year round.

Preparation and care

The golden rule, whether collecting flowers from your garden or buying them from a florist, is to do so early in the day. At this time it is cooler so garden flowers are at their best while, as far as the florist is concerned, the flowers are more likely to be fresh.

CHOOSING SUNFLOWERS

Sunflowers should only be bought, or cut, when the petals are fully open. Check that the foliage is firm, and that there is no pollen on the seeds – if there is, it indicates that the flowers are past their best.

When selecting cut flowers, avoid those wrapped in cellophane as this speeds up the process of decay. Be sure that the flower buckets are sheltered from direct sunlight and the water is fresh and clear; if it is stale and smelly, the flowers have obviously been sitting in it for some time.

TRIMMING AND CONDITIONING

Correct preparation is vital for prolonging a flower's life and ensuring it looks its best. If collecting flowers from the garden, take a bucket of water with you, ready to put them straight in. Once inside, use a sharp knife or pruning shears to cut the stems at an angle, trimming them by a minimum of 1 in/2.5 cm. For best results, do this underwater to stop air being taken up the stem.

Bought flowers should be trimmed in the same way. Once trimmed, the flowers should be left to stand in a bucket of water in a cool, shady spot for a minimum of three hours. This gives them time to suck up a good supply of water to their heads – vital to avoid droop and wilting leaves. Of course, the taller the stem, the longer this process takes.

If your sunflower is looking droopy, a good method of reviving it is to lay the whole flower flat in a bath of tepid water. Before arranging, strip all foliage off the stems below the water level.

ONGOING CARE

A basic rule is to use cool water, to change it frequently (every couple of days), and to remove decaying material. When changing the water, do not remove the flowers and refill the container, as this allows the flowers to take up too much air. Instead, place the whole arrangement in the sink and run the tap until all the old water has been washed out and replaced by the fresh.

At each change of water, trim another ½ in/1 cm off the stem. You can also add flower food to the water at each water change. This fights bacteria as well as providing nutrients and acidifier, making the flowers last longer and necessitating fewer water changes. Flower food is readily available in sachets from florists, or you could try home-made: mix together equal parts of water and lemonade, and add a drop of bleach. Flower food will discolor the water, so do not use in clear glass vases. Avoid placing your flowers anywhere too hot, such as near a stove or in direct sunlight, and also avoid drafts.

If your arrangement is held in florist's foam (oasis), then you need to take special care when watering so as not to disturb it. Ensure your container holding the foam is large enough to hold some extra water, and top this off regularly.

More complicated designs, such as swags or balls, need special treatment. To water these, mist frequently, using a pump-action spray, available at any hardware shop or garden center.

One of the joys of dried flower arrangements is that once you have gone to the effort of putting them together, maintenance couldn't be easier. All you have to do to keep them looking their best is to avoid placing them in direct sunlight, as this fades colors quite dramatically, and lightly blow off any dust that has accumulated.

'Pastiche' (left), is easy to grow, and ideal for flower arrangements.

'Sunflowers' (right), by Elizabeth Jane Lloyd.

Which container?

Choosing a container provides the opportunity to allow one's imagination to run wild. Anything capable of holding water can be used for flowers; however, there are a few general points worth bearing in mind.

First, the container should not detract in any way from the planned arrangement. On the most basic level, it should not clash or distract colorwise, and should be a suitable shape. As sunflowers are tall, they usually need a tall container, preferably with a narrow neck to support their stems, although florist's foam (oasis), and wire, will help you to circumvent this if you are aiming for a particular look. You could also use a container within a container, to help give support to your arrangement.

Another consideration is the water rule. Long stemmed flowers such as sunflowers need plenty of water, so you must be able to refill your chosen container easily. Bearing all of this in mind, there are still a huge number of styles and shapes of container in which sunflowers look spectacular.

①
②
③
④

① CONTEMPORARY

There are many modern containers which suit sunflower arrangements. Bold, dramatic sunflowers look very striking in simple, modern vases, and this is appropriate for today's modern-style homes. Metal finish and glass vases can look stunning. Frosted glass has a rather mysterious feel, while plain glass creates a shimmering effect.

② PEASANT

For a natural, earthy look reminiscent of the Mediterranean, large terracotta pots, looking like small pithoi, are ideal. Sunflowers are among the few flowers tall enough for such pots. Similarly, look out for simple luster-ware jugs and part-glazed, rough-finished peasant jugs. These often have a hint of green which goes beautifully with the sunflower's foliage and helps create a wonderful, warm Provençal feel.

③ GRAND

A small urn, possibly on a pedestal or table, in a hall or fireplace, makes a very unexpected container for sunflowers. However humble they may be, sunflowers have the stature and bearing not to look out of place in such an august receptacle, while any contrast between the stateliness of the urn, and the simplicity of the sunflowers is irresistible.

④ COUNTRY

A plastic-lined basket looks wonderfully rural filled with sunflowers, especially when overflowing with an abundance of foliage and other seasonal flowers. If planned well the arrangement should look as though it has grown out of the brown wickerwork.

⑤ WILD AND WACKY

Geometric, 50s-style vases make fabulous containers. The sunflowers' bright, open faces work especially well with the somewhat naive designs of this period. Simple monochrome patterns are particularly effective.

⑥ RUSTIC

Comb thrift shops for old terracotta or stoneware pots used to store beer and cider. Their dull brown color complements the sunflowers' vivid yellows and oranges. Dark green 'cabbage leaf' jugs also look extremely attractive filled with golden-yellow sunflowers.

Fresh flower arrangements

Sunflowers are becoming more widely available as cut flowers, as their popularity grows. They are long-lasting (7-10 days in a vase), and make fabulous, bold arrangements, irresistibly drawing the eye with their large blooms and bright colors. The traditional, single, annual sunflowers appear in the late summer to early autumn, when they are particularly valuable, there being so few brightly colored blooms still around. However, the perennial sprays are available from early summer.

There are many factors to consider when planning a flower arrangement. Start by considering the occasion, container and surroundings. It must not overwhelm, or be overwhelmed by, its setting. For example, a natural-looking design which looks as though it has just been thrust – albeit artfully – into a vase, will be out of place in a very formal room.

Color, texture and perfume are also considerations. Colors can have a dramatic impact on the feel of an arrangement. Hot colors (those in the red spectrum), draw the eye and create a lively, busy feel, while cool colors (those in the blue spectrum), engender an atmosphere of quiet tranquillity. The texture of petals, leaves and stalks varies enormously from plant to plant, and adds dimension to an arrangement. Consider scent; it would be quite disastrous, for example, to make up a centrepiece of flowers bursting with heady aromas on a supper table.

The best advice for beginners, is to keep it simple. Overambitious arrangements are more likely, at best, to miss the mark, or, in the worst case, look frightfully out of place.

Sunflowers can be cut short, but they look best left with long stems: their height is part of their charm. So keep a sense of proportion and bear in mind that although some flowers may look attractive cut short, sunflowers could look sadly truncated.

Fill a yellow and orange vase for your own Vincent Van Gogh. Include some sunflowers which are not yet fully open, for an authentic look.

A LA VAN GOGH

You will be very lucky to find a ready-painted orange and yellow vase, so why not paint your own? Any wooden or earthenware vase would work, but terracotta would be best. You will only need to buy small sample pots of emulsion paint from your local hardware store. There is no need to prepare the surface; a rough surface will only add to the charm. And you won't need to varnish your pot either!

Choose any sunflowers that you like. Van Gogh painted a series of sunflower paintings, and the sunflowers vary in all of them. 'Sunburst', 'Teddy Bear' and 'Pastiche' would make a good start. The arrangement could not be simpler: start with the tallest sunflowers, and arrange smaller sunflowers and buds around. And there you have it – your very own Van Gogh masterpiece!

NATURAL

A tall, plain, blue vase bursting with sunflowers captures the very essence of summer – blue skies and golden sunshine. Blue and yellow are perfect companions, seen time and time again in nature, and will liven up a summer lunch party or sit happily in the centre of the kitchen table.

For a relaxed occasion such as an informal *al fresco* meal, a few sunflowers on their own is all that is needed – anything else would seem overstated.

'Cut Flower Mixture' is a flower arranger's dream. It lasts well and comes in many colors.

'Sunburst' is available in several colors, and is easily grown in a domestic garden.

A perfect
al fresco
centerpiece.

Sunflowers work well in simple, contemporary vases.

CONTEMPORARY

Sunflowers in a clear, glass vase with some cow parsley, irises, a few fern fronds, and perhaps some ivy trailing over the sides, will create a really strong, sophisticated look, perfect for a modern house or city apartment.

For another very modern look, mix sunflowers with *Eryngium alpinum* (sea holly). These mysterious-looking flowers, with their beautiful, light blue, fluffy bracts surrounding long 'cones' have a fabulously feathery appearance – an excellent contrast to the woodiness of the sunflowers. However, anyone tempted to stroke these wonderfully tactile flowers will get a prickly surprise. This combination will look spectacular in a plain glass or terracotta vase.

Team sunflowers up with bamboo, papyrus, dasylirion (bear grass), fennel flowers, euphorbia (spurge) and flat-headed achillea (yarrow) for an exotic look with a touch of the jungle. To get the best from this arrangement, choose a large, deep, ethnic type of container, such as an Indian beaten copper dish or an African clay water carrier.

FORMAL

Sunflowers may not be considered grand flowers, but their lofty stature makes them naturally imposing and able to hold their own at the smartest supper party or reception.

For an elegant, extravagant display, place them in an urn or other grand-looking container with luscious roses and alstroemeria. You could also use graceful *Moluccella* (bells of Ireland, also known as shell flower) or euphorbia (spurge), but take care not to get any of the irritating sap on your skin. A collar of hosta leaves will contrast wonderfully with the tall, thin sunflowers and *Moluccella*, as well as hiding any ugly stems. As urns have wide necks, you will need to use scrunched up balls of chicken wire or wire mesh to keep the flowers in position.

Sunflowers add stature to a formal arrangement.

Bring the fruits of the earth into your home.

LATE SUMMER FEAST

Create an extravagant, but informal display for a hall table or sideboard, using a low, wide, plastic-lined basket and florist's foam (oasis) or wire.

The key to the success of this display is to choose flowers which look as though they have just been picked from a country garden and to arrange them so that they splay out of the basket in a cascade of color. While those living in the country may be lucky enough to have a large garden and to be able to pick their flowers, city dwellers have to be content with creating the impression that they have done so.

Combine sunflowers with tall spikes of any of the following: *Solidago* (golden rod), gentians, *Echinops*, penstemons, scabious, salvia (sage), asters, cornflowers, phlox, marguerites, anemones and *Antirrhinums* – all are perfect.

FLEMISH OPULENCE

This style looks particularly dramatic in an old house or darkish corner of a room, where the vibrant colors will positively glow. Use an urn or similar container filled with crumpled chicken wire to hold the stems.

The basic idea is to create a classic, tall, dome-shaped arrangement using warm, luxurious colors, such as yellows, oranges and reds, but with a touch of purple-blue to help emphasise the richness of the other colors.

For the purple-blue, irises and agapanthus (African lily), being tall and straight, are perfect, while sunflowers, lilies, rudbeckias (coneflowers), and crocosmia (monbretia), can provide the shades of gold, and anenomes, poppies, mop-headed hydrangeas, zinnias and nicotiana the reds. Be sure to include tulips for the Dutch feel.

BURST OF HOT COLORS

It can get a little dull being tasteful all the time, so, as an antidote to beautifully co-ordinated colors, try something bold and flamboyant. It is worth experimenting with combinations of bold, brassy-colored flowers (see page 35).

While the idea of placing vibrant oranges, yellows, purples and reds side-by-side may seem alarming, the result is actually quite spectacular. If the colors are sufficiently intense, a form of magic takes place whereby combinations that one would expect to clash, actually look glorios with tremendous vitality. There are many vivid companions for sunflowers; experiment with bold anemones, gerberas, nasturtiums and dahlias.

A word of warning, though: choose a dull, sombre-colored container, preferably with a simple shape, otherwise the overall effect could be too overwhelming.

DAISY CHAIN

Mix sunflowers with other daisy-like flowers for a really starry display. Choose yellow varieties of anthemis (chamomile), heliopsis, helenium (sneezewort), gerbera and *Argyranthemum frutescens* (marguerite) as well as the sunflower's smaller relative, the rudbeckia (coneflower). A particularly good species is *Rudbeckia fulgida* var. *deamii*, as their delicate flowers with long droopy petals and dark centres echo the sunflowers'.

For a really dazzling, spontaneous effect, stick to similar shades of yellow and gold, and even continue the theme with the foliage – variegated privet and elaeagnus are ideal.

FRUITS OF THE EARTH

Late summer, with its hints of short, autumn days to come, is a curious time. There is sadness at the end of summer, but also excitement and anticipation at the coming of a new season.

Many countries have festivals at this time: harvest festivals in Europe, Labor Day and Thanksgiving in America. It is a time worth celebrating, so plan a feast and create a spectacular centrepiece for your table.

Surround sunflowers (themselves a crop), with orangey-red chinese lanterns and rose hips. Around these group a selection of colorful squash and the most attractive, fresh, seasonal fruit and vegetables; such as globe artichokes, glossy aubergines, golden corncobs, split pomegranates and grapes.

To represent the changing season include some turning tree foliage. The reds and bronzes will act as a perfect foil for the sunflowers' vibrant yellow.

Sunflowers add welcome cheer.

Dried flower arrangements

Dried flowers allow us to cheat on nature by combining flowers from different seasons – flowers that could never grow naturally side-by-side in a garden. For example, pretty little spring flowers can sit with those of late summer. The results are very striking and are guaranteed to grab and hold people's attention, without them even realising quite why they are so drawn.

When planning an arrangement using dried sunflowers (see page 28), remember that they look very different from fresh flowers. For example, the brightly-colored petals, especially the yellows, will be less vivid, while the center of the flower will appear darker. Also the petals shrivel slightly when dried so seem smaller in relation to the seedhead. Yet these are not disadvantages as, for example, smaller petals allow us to see the beautiful seed structure more clearly.

Overall, the dried flower looks wonderfully rich, yet mellow; a piece of summer preserved to enjoy throughout the winter.

PRETTY AND SCENTED

A very attractive style for a bedroom is a tiered arrangement, sometimes known as a 'stepped mass'. Cut a piece of florist's foam (oasis), to fit in a large flowerpot. Select a few sunflowers (the exact number will depend on the size of pot, but should be odd), and wire their heads around one thin cane – this makes it easier to insert them into the foam and also allows you to tilt their heads. Then surround with a slightly shorter, deeper circle of poppy heads, then another circle, shorter and deeper still, of lavender bunches, preferably the spectacular, blue *Lavandula stoechas* (French lavender). The massed ranks of the poppy heads and lavender, so stiffly standing to attention, provide a wonderful contrast to the flat, spreading, rather dishevelled, aspect of the sunflower at their summit. Finish with a fringe of sphagnum moss, pinned in place to soften the edges and hide the foam. A ribbon tied in a bow around the flowerpot will complete the picture.

TALL AND STATELY

Sunflowers and *Cynara scolymus* (globe artichoke), look tremendously stylish together. Like sunflowers, the globe artichoke is a crop as well as being a thing of beauty in its own right. Surround these lofty companions with a frill of *Alchemilla mollis* (lady's mantle). The delicate alchemilla gives a lovely soft feel, and contrasts well with the dramatic and robust-looking sunflowers and artichokes – both with their large heavy heads. If you cannot track down a globe artichoke, a similar effect can be achieved with *Echinops* (globe thistle), which is also tall with an unusual rounded head. For a variation with more color, add elegant delphiniums and campanula. Be sure to mass

the finer flowers for a strong effect – single stems will look lost and out-of-scale among the heavier sunflowers and globe artichokes.

COOK'S SWAG

Swags look wonderful hanging from the mantelpiece, over doorways or above beds. Although there are infinite possible flowers and foliage which will look good with sunflowers, and work well in swags, it is best to avoid being over-ambitious at first. Instead, start off with a short swag, keeping the design simple. For a strong theme, look to the kitchen for inspiration and concoct a culinary treat.

Many herbs, besides being delicious and fragrant, are pretty, and as sunflowers are also used for food, why not combine them and make a useful, and attractive small swag to hang in the kitchen. If the cook finds he or she has run out of anything, they could always raid the swag. Bay leaves, rosemary, mint, oregano and marjoram would look very effective because the purple and green colors predominant among these herbs work beautifully with the yellow sunflowers.

You can add another splash of color with small bunches of red hot, or cool green chilies. A small string of onions or garlic, hanging down vertically at either end of the swag would also be a useful touch. Besides sunflowers, you could feature marigolds and nasturtiums in your swag to provide another touch of gold – and both are edible when fresh.

METHOD

1 Start by assembling, bunching and wiring your small ingredients, such as the herbs.
2 Cut out an oblong of chicken wire the size you want your swag to be.
3 Lay the wire flat and fill with sphagnum moss, then bend it up until the sides meet to form a sausage shape. Join the edges with reel wire, then pinch either end of the sausage until slightly tapered, which gives a well-finished appearance. Stuff with extra moss if necessary, until happy with the shape.

4 Begin to decorate the swag, aiming to keep the swag balanced in terms of weight and color. Start with your sunflowers in the central part of your swag (being the largest elements of the swag and relatively heavy). You may find it easier to work with the swag lying on a flat surface rather than hanging up. Simply attach your 'ingredients' onto the main wire mesh, using floral wire.
5 Next, add your foliage (e.g. the leafy herbs), and any flowered herbs and chilies.
6 If you decide to add strings of onions and garlic, add them when the swag is in its permanent position, because they are heavy. Be sure that they look as though they are part of the swag or the effect will be spoilt. For a natural look, use raffia to hang the swag and to attach any onions or garlic.

Dried sunflowers are a piece of summer preserved to enjoy year-round.

Dried flower wreath

There is something very special about a wreath. Maybe it is because a circle is such a satisfying shape – being complete, and without a beginning or an end. Or, it could be because it is a shape found so often in nature. One of the best things about dried flower wreaths is that they look impressively professional, yet are actually very easy to make. You simply add seasonal, dried flowers of your choice, until you are happy with the final result.

MATERIALS

❀ hay or twig ring to use as your base (you can buy this from any good florists) ❀ stub (floral) wire ❀ gutta-percha tape ❀ a selection of flowers, foliage, nuts and berries depending on the season ❀ imagination

SUMMER WREATH: select classic summer flowers, such as roses, nigella (love-in-a-mist), and delphiniums. Add lavender and *Centaurea* (cornflowers), for delicious shades of blue, which will look wonderful with dried sunflowers.

AUTUMN WREATH: use golden ears of corn and bunches of oats as the base. Add canary grass, *Papaver* (poppy) seedheads and thistles for texture. You can buy many of these ready-dyed, or you could try dying or spraying your materials to ring the changes.

METHOD

1 Start by planning your design on the ground. Lay out your bunches of flowers and foliage in a circle and stand back. Take a hard look at the colors and shapes, then work out a rough design. By doing this, you will get a good, overall feel, and be able to see how much of each material you have. It is important to avoid the disastrous situation of finding that you've run out of something halfway around the circle, creating a dreadful lopsided effect.

2 Next, sort out the flowers and foliage which need to be wired into bunches. The strength of the stem and the size of the flower head will determine this. You will need to wire any fragile, or small, or broken-stemmed flowers or seedheads (see page 28). Simply bind a wire to the stem with gutta-percha tape. Gutta-percha comes in a range of natural colors, and will blend into your arrangement. Tape your foliage (oats, corn etc.) into small bunches.

3 Next, start to build up the wreath. There are various methods of attaching the flowers to the wreath. Flowers with tough stems can be pushed into the ring and large-headed flowers can even be glued on. However, the best method is to use a length of thin spool (reel) wire to secure material. Wrap the wire around the stem or bunch, then push through the ring and twist at the back to secure.

4 Start with your foliage first, and work around the ring so the material follows in the same direction. Add the sunflowers next, as they are the largest flower in your design and also the focus, so any additional material serves to highlight them. Finally, add your smaller material, continuing to follow the line of the foliage.

5 To mount your wreath, attach a piece of florist's wire to the back of the wreath in a loop. The wreath is actually fairly light, so you will not need anything stronger. Then stand back and admire your work!

Cooking with sunflowers

Sunflower seeds are extremely versatile. They can be eaten roasted and salted as a snack, or baked in breads and biscuits, or used as a tasty garnish for salads. As well as being delicious, they also provide a wealth of nutrition and energy. Their delicious flavors and health-giving properties are just what you would expect from a plant so closely linked with the life-giving sun. So, don your apron and let these recipes, using this most versatile of plants, inspire you to create a sunshine feast.

Sunflower products and properties

Throughout the world, but especially in Eastern Europe, the Mediterranean countries and across North America, great fields of sunflowers raise their heads to the sky every year. Millions of acres are dedicated to growing sunflowers, and obviously, they are grown for more than their beauty. Sunflowers are a very important crop, and they have been grown for their seeds for centuries.

It was the native peoples of the Americas who first realized the massive potential of this lovely plant and began to exploit it fully, using sunflowers to make food, dyes and fiber.

Nowadays sunflowers are grown especially for the oil the seeds yield when crushed. Sunflowers are the fifth largest oilseed crop in the world, producing a high-grade cooking oil, which is used in its natural state for cooking, or processed into margarines.

Sunflower oil is not only used for cooking, it is an important ingredient in a whole range of products, from diesel to paint, from plastic to varnish. Every part of the plant can be used for something – even the pith is pressed into service in the manufacture of buoyancy aids such as life jackets and belts – being an amazing ten times lighter than cork. Any spent plant is not wasted, but made into silage.

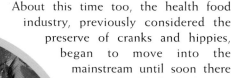
Sunflower oil is delicious *and* good for you.

Sunflower seeds are also a very important crop. Birds love them

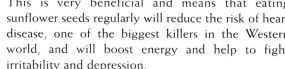

and they are a vital addition to most birdseed mixes – 'Peredovik' being the most popular variety grown for this use. Besides birds, humans also like to snack on these tasty seeds and they are extremely useful in cooking, either used straight or sprouted.

By the seventies, the rise in health problems caused by the West's increasing reliance on highly processed foods led to a desire to rediscover a simpler, more natural diet. As people started to take more of an interest in what they ate, they gradually became aware of the dangers posed by fats and cholesterol and looked for foods that could be used to counteract this threat.

About this time too, the health food industry, previously considered the preserve of cranks and hippies, began to move into the mainstream until soon there was a health food shop in every main street. With this rapid expansion of the industry, a wider range of people began to realize the healthy properties of sunflower seeds, and so demand for them soared.

Rightly so, because sunflower seeds have high levels of B group vitamins (iodine and phosphorus), protein, minerals and fiber, but most beneficial of all, they are high in linoleic acid, a polyunsaturated fatty acid. This is important because polyunsaturated fats lower the level of cholesterol in the blood, thereby reducing the risk of heart disease. This is very beneficial and means that eating sunflower seeds regularly will reduce the risk of heart disease, one of the biggest killers in the Western world, and will boost energy and help to fight irritability and depression.

SUNFLOWER SEED SPROUTS

Every schoolchild will be familiar with sprouting seeds as they are the most common example used to teach children about the wonders of germination. As one can gather from this, they are very simple to sprout, not to mention cheap.

Sprouts are deliciously crunchy so make excellent additions to salads. They are also ideal for

Palestine or Jerusalem artichoke soup

SERVES 4

This is a rich, thick soup which, when served with warmed Italian ciabatta or olive bread, is a meal in itself. It is a simple dish to prepare and cook. In fact the hardest part of the preparation is scrubbing or peeling the artichokes – quite a time-consuming job due to their knobbly shape.

2 lb/900 g Jerusalem artichokes, peeled or well scrubbed
juice of 1 lemon
1 tablespoon sunflower margarine
1 medium onion, peeled and chopped
1/2 pint/1 cup milk
1 pint/2 cups chicken stock
salt and freshly ground black pepper, to taste
1 tablespoon chopped parsley, to garnish

1 Peel the artichokes and cut into small chunks.
2 Place in a pan of cold water with the lemon juice and set to boil.
3 While the artichokes are cooking, lightly fry the onion in the sunflower margarine.
4 Once the artichokes are soft, allow them to cool, and then drain, saving the water they have been cooked in.
5 Place the artichokes, onions, milk and stock in a blender, season and pureé.
6 As you pureé, slowly add the cooking water until the soup becomes the consistency you want, then reheat, season to taste, and serve with a sprinkling of parsley, to garnish.

Pumpkin soup

SERVES 4

Sunflowers and squashes are companion plants in the garden, so it makes sense to continue that partnership into the kitchen. This wonderfully thick, creamy soup will warm up a cold day without being over-rich. Serve with hunks of oven-warmed French pain de campagne or Italian ciabatta.

1 1/2 lb/750 g pumpkin
2 tablespoons sunflower oil
3 medium sized onions, chopped
2 garlic cloves, crushed
pinch of cayenne pepper
1/2 teaspoon ground cumin
1 bay leaf
1 pint/2 cups vegetable stock
1/4 pint/2/3 cup single cream
freshly ground black pepper

1 Chop the pumpkin into quarters and cut away the flesh from the hard skin. Discard the seeds and cut the flesh into cubes.
2 Heat the sunflower oil in a large pan and add the onion, garlic, spices and bay leaf, then cook over a low heat until soft.
3 Slowly add the pumpkin and cook, gently stirring, until it starts to turn pulpy, then pour in the stock. Season and cover.
4 Leave to simmer for at least an hour, then pureé.
5 Once smooth, pour the soup back into the pan. Add the cream, and gently reheat to serve. Season with freshly ground black pepper to taste.

Sunflower date bread

SERVES 4

This dense, tasty bake makes a delicious teatime treat. Cut it into thick slices and serve with a good, thick coating of sunflower margarine or butter.

4 tablespoons sunflower margarine
4 oz/¹/₂ cup soft brown sugar
¹/₂ pint/1 cup milk
6 oz/³/₄ cup dates, pitted and chopped
4 oz/¹/₂ cup plain flour
4 oz/¹/₂ cup wholemeal flour
1¹/₂ teaspoons baking powder
pinch of salt
3 oz/¹/₃ cup sunflower seeds
1 medium egg, beaten

1 Melt the sunflower spread and sugar in a pan over a low heat, then add the milk and dates and warm through. Keep the mixture warm over a very low heat, but do not allow the mixture to boil.
2 Sift the flour and baking powder into a bowl then add the pinch of salt and the sunflower seeds. Add the egg and combine thoroughly.
3 Add the milk mixture to the bowl and roughly mix.
4 Pour the mixture into a greased, lined loaf tin, and cook in a preheated oven at 350°F/175°C for 35-40 minutes. To check it is cooked, insert a skewer or knife into the middle, and if it comes out clean, the bread is done. This is delicious served slightly warm, or cold.

Using petals

Petals are now widely used in cookery. They make tasty and pretty additions to salads and desserts. However, sunflower petals are deadly poisonous, so do not be tempted to use them. However, if you want to maintain a sunflower theme for a special occasion, it is possible to cheat. Yellow nasturtium petals look almost exactly the same as yellow sunflower petals, and are the most widely used petal for cookery.

You could use nasturtium petals as a pretty and unusual garnish for a green salad, or for the Summer Tabbouleh recipe (on page 55). You can also use them to decorate iced cakes, desserts and drinks.

Petal-filled ice cubes are very unusual and effective, yet are child's play to make. Simply fill an ice cube tray with water and drop a nasturtium petal into each compartment, then place in the freezer until solid. The resulting cubes, each with their tiny portion of captured sunshine, look spectacular floating in a clear jug of home-made lemonade, a tall glass of sparkling water, or a glass of ice-cold Pimm's.

Feeding pets and wildlife

Many people put out food for animals and birds to tide them over the lean times, or simply to attract a variety of wildlife to the garden in order to observe their antics. Either way it is an extremely worthwhile pursuit and one guaranteed to provide hours of pleasure.

If you are worried about the welfare of birds and animals, you will probably already put food out during the harsh winter months. However, few people realize spring can be an extremely difficult time for wild animals and birds. This is because there tends to be a period when the new fruits, seed heads and insects haven't yet appeared. Similarly, a hot summer may deprive wildlife as bone dry ground will prevent insects from emerging.

Sunflower seeds can provide an answer to these problems. In winter and early spring, make seed and nut cakes for birds and mice, or in late summer provide a ready-made feast by cutting off sunflower seedheads when they are ripe and hanging them up around the garden. You will be staggered at how many species you will attract. However, sunflower seeds are very rich, so do not put too many out at any one time. Among the many varieties of sunflower guaranteed to thrill birds and animals are 'Peredovik', 'Sundak' and 'Arrowhead'.

Pets also appreciate sunflower seeds. Hamsters, gerbils and guinea pigs will all be delighted by a sunflower seed treat – in fact sunflower seeds are gerbils' and hamsters' favorite titbit (as well as being very good for them).

Bird seed cake

You can use any mix of fat, seeds and nuts that you like. The quantities are flexible – just use what kitchen scraps you have. Aim to make a cake the size of a tennis ball.

selection of fats – such as suet, bacon fat, lard or
dripping from roast meat
sunflower seeds
selection of nuts, well chopped

1 Mix all the fats together and knead into a ball.
2 Roll the fat ball in the seeds and nuts, thoroughly coating it.
3 Using a long, thick, carpet darning needle, thread twine through the center of the ball.
4 Tie a knot in one end of the twine and fashion a loop in the other end. Your bird seed cake is now ready to hang in the garden.

Home-made hamster and gerbil mix

Commercial pet food mixes can be expensive, so if you have a crop of sunflower seeds, you could make your own. A mature hamster or gerbil will eat about one tablespoon of this mix a day.

you need equal amounts of the following:
sunflower seeds
oats, wheat or millet
peanuts

1 Simply mix all the ingredients together. Store the mixture in a well-sealed tin in a cool, dry place.

Salad oils and dressings

Salad dressing either makes or breaks a salad. Anything too strong or too sharp will kill the delicate flavors of the leaves, yet the dressing must not be too bland as it gives the salad its character. In other words, the cook must perform a delicate balancing act.

Different oils have different characteristics. For example, extra virgin olive oil has a fruity flavor, while many other oils are nutty. Sunflower oil has a light, delicate flavor, which makes it ideal for use in a dressing. It is also ideal for mixing with olive oil because it tones down the latter's strong flavor to make a lighter dressing, or used on its own, it goes well with more distinctive flavors, such as lime.

The mildness of sunflower oil makes it an excellent base for the subtle flavors characteristic of infused oils. Making infusions, or flavored oils, is very simple and very satisfying, and is an excellent way of increasing your range of oils at virtually no cost. The result will be heavenly. In fact, in some cases, as with basil for example, the herb flavor is so strong that you can use an infused oil straight as a salad dressing. The best sunflower oil to use for these recipes is one from the 'first pressing', which is usually clearly labeled on the bottle.

If you use a variety of bottles your oils will also look extremely decorative. A shelf beside a stove filled with a collection of different sized, shaped and colored bottles each filled with a unique oil not only looks beautiful but is appetizing and an inspiration to any cook. And with the key ingredient floating in the oil for all to see, you don't even need to spoil the bottle with a label.

Any, or a mixture of the following, can be added to sunflower oil:

HERBS •rosemary •French tarragon •basil •thyme

SPICES •garlic •peppercorns •ginger •fresh chilies

1 Half fill a sterilized bottle with your choice of herbs and spices.
2 Pour in the sunflower oil, filling to the top.
3 Seal and leave for a couple of weeks to allow the flavors to infuse into the oil.

Quick French dressing

❁

3 tablespoons sunflower oil
3 tablespoons extra virgin olive oil
2 tablespoons wine vinegar
1 tablespoon smooth Dijon mustard
freshly ground black pepper

1 Place all the ingredients in a small, screw-top, glass jar or blender and mix well.
2 Shake the jar well to combine all the ingredients and create a thick, smooth dressing with a lovely, strong, mustard kick.

Sunshine lemon dressing

2 tablespoons sunflower oil
2 tablespoons lemon juice
pinch of finely-grated lemon rind
sugar, to taste
salt and pepper, to taste

1 Place the oil and lemon juice in a small, screw-top glass jar or blender and mix well.
2 Stir in the lemon rind then add sugar and seasoning to taste.

Sweet lime dressing

Limes are often overlooked as a dressing ingredient, which is a great pity as they have a marvelous flavor, especially when, as here, you add a hint of sweetness. This dressing will work wonderfully with seafood, as well as on plain green salads.

4 tablespoons sunflower oil
1 garlic clove, crushed
1 teaspoon light brown sugar
juice of 1 lime

1 Place the oil, garlic and sugar in a small, screw-top glass jar or blender and mix well.
2 Pour in the lime juice, and mix again.
3 Taste the dressing, and add more sugar to taste.

Why not try making your own infusion? Clockwise from top: sunflower oil with rosemary; sunflower oil with garlic, paprika and chilies; sunflower oil with chilies, tarragon and paprika.

Sunflower directory

The sunflower family consists of more than 150 varieties, with perennials as well as annuals, and there are as many as ten new breeds being introduced each year. They bear large, daisy-like flowers in summer and autumn, the majority of which are shades of yellow. Besides being deservedly popular among gardeners, they are a vital crop, grown for their seeds and oil which are used for foodstuffs as well as for industry.

Sunflowers are simple to grow, preferring a well-drained soil and plenty of sunshine. Almost all are fully hardy and the perennials can be invasive. They are easily grown from home-grown seed although perennials can also be propagated by division.

Annuals

Among the enormous variety of sunflowers, the annuals make up the largest group. There are more than one hundred varieties among which there are dwarfs as well as giants, although the majority of annual sunflowers are tall with single heads.

Single blooms

The most popular sunflowers of all, many of the varieties produce edible seeds, loved by birds and humans alike.

African Sunset

PLANT HEIGHT:
4-5 ft/1.2-1.5 m
IDEAL FOR:
bird food, border planting, flower arranging

HELIANTHUS ANNUUS

A brand-new variety, 'African Sunset' comes in a mixture of colors as dazzling as its name. There are smooth creamy-whites, sunny yellows, vivid oranges, rich reds as well as deep mahoganies. The 4-6 in/ 10-15 cm blooms look stupendous in a border, but also last extremely well once cut. The flowers also yield a mass of seeds, which can be saved for replanting or left as a feast to attract birds. One of the biggest advantages of this variety is that the seeds grow happily planted directly into the garden.

Arrowhead

HELIANTHUS ANNUUS

PLANT HEIGHT:
6 ft/1.8 m
IDEAL FOR:
bird food

This is mainly grown commercially for seed, however, there is no reason why it cannot be grown in the garden. Birds love the seeds, so be sure to protect your sunflowers (see pages 24-5). A traditional, mid-yellow sunflower.

Autumn Beauty

HELIANTHUS ANNUUS

PLANT HEIGHT:
4-6 ft/1.2-1.8 m
IDEAL FOR:
bird food, flower arranging, screen

A popular, widely-available variety which is multi-branching and bears bold blooms in pink, gold, lemon-yellow, bronze and mahogany-red. Some of 'Autumn Beauty's' 8 in/20 cm flowers are bi-colored. It is good to plant as a screen, and for cutting. Birds adore the seeds. It has a good, long flowering period – from July to October.

AUTUMN BEAUTY

Aztec Gold

PLANT HEIGHT:
6 ft/1.8 m
IDEAL FOR:
bird food, crop, focal point, screen

HELIANTHUS ANNUUS

The enormous (11 in/28 cm), seedheads on this tall sunflower yield the most delicious, fat, edible seeds. They are ideal for using in cookery (see Cooking with Sunflowers, page 50).

This variety, with its sunny yellow petals looks dramatic if grown as a focal point, but also works extremely well as a screen. Be sure to net your sunflower if you are growing it as a crop, otherwise the birds will move in and strip it in a flash.

Big Smile

HELIANTHUS ANNUUS

PLANT HEIGHT:
1-2 ft/30-60 cm
IDEAL FOR:
border planting, children, containers

This cheerful, dwarf plant has deep golden-yellow flowers (3-4 in/8-10 cm) with lovely, very dark orange centres. It is perfectly happy in containers, and will look stunning grouped on a terrace, but if you want it to grow taller, then plant it in a border. It is a wonderful variety for a children's garden. 'Big Smile' flowers from July through to August.

BIG SMILE

Chianti Hybrid

HELIANTHUS ANNUUS

PLANT HEIGHT:
4-5 ft/1.2-1.5 m

IDEAL FOR:
flower arranging, focal point

This new variety features multi-branching purple stems bearing the most astonishing, deep, rich wine-red blooms with even darker, almost black, centres. These dramatic 3-4 in/8-10 cm flowers have petals flecked with gold and are pollenless so are perfect for cutting.

CHILD'S PLAYHOUSE (SEE PAGE 17)

Color Fashion Mix

HELIANTHUS ANNUUS

PLANT HEIGHT:
6 ft/1.8 m

IDEAL FOR:
border planting, flower arranging, screen

As its name suggests, this variety is all about color, in this case a heady mix of reds and yellows with some jazzy purple thrown in for good measure. These lovely shades make 'Color Fashion Mix' a fabulous choice for anyone keen on flower arranging, and added to its height means they will look stupendous at the back of a border, as a screen, or framing a gate or doorway.

Common Sunflower

HELIANTHUS ANNUUS

PLANT HEIGHT:
3-9 ft/90 cm-2.7 m

IDEAL FOR:
border planting, crop, focal point

This is the traditional, upright sunflower which everyone knows and loves. Flowering mid- to late-summer, it is an integral part of the Mediterranean landscape and has inspired artists for centuries. Prefering light, well-drained soil, the 'Common Sunflower' is an easy plant which is very fast-growing and bears large (1 ft/30 cm), yellow blooms with purple or dark brown centres above mid-green leaves.

Cucumber-leaf Sunflower

HELIANTHUS DEBILIS

PLANT HEIGHT:
3-5 ft/90 cm-1.5 m

IDEAL FOR:
flower arranging, screen

'Cucumber-leaf Sunflower' (see overleaf), stands gloriously erect, with its many branches producing distinctive 3 in/8 cm yellow flowers with maroon and red-brown centres. Its particular feature is its lovely, glossy, green leaves. As it has a wonderfully long flowering period (from July to September), it makes a perfect screen to hide eyesores, such as a compost heap or oil tank. It also lasts well once cut so is ideal for arrangements.

CUCUMBER-LEAF SUNFLOWER (SEE PAGE 67)

Cut Flower Mixture

HELIANTHUS ANNUUS

PLANT HEIGHT:
4-5 ft/1.2-1.5 m
IDEAL FOR:
flower arranging

The blooms of 'Cut Flower Mixture' come in various shades from lemon to bronze. As its name suggests, the flowers are excellent for arrangements. This variety is notable for its large flower heads which produce masses of seeds. It flowers from July to September.

Discovery Mix

HELIANTHUS ANNUUS

PLANT HEIGHT:
8 ft/2.4 m
IDEAL FOR:
border planting

An excellent variety providing a huge range of colors and combinations – from golden-orange to lemon-yellow and bi-colored orange and brown. Some of the medium-sized flowers (6 in/15 cm), are semi-double, and all have different colored centres – from orange to a deep, rich brown. 'Discovery Mix' produces anything up to 6-15 branches.

Endurance

**HELIANTHUS ARGOPHYLLUS
X ANNUUS**

PLANT HEIGHT:
6-9 ft/1.8-2.7 m
IDEAL FOR:
flower arranging

'Endurance' is one of the brand new varieties. It is very prolific, producing small-centred, large-petalled, bright yellow flowers about 4-6 in/10-15 cm in diameter. Each plant grows an astonishing 50 branches, each ending in a cluster of 2-5 long-lasting flowers. The stiff stems, multi-branching habit and number of blooms makes 'Endurance' an ideal sunflower for the flower arranger.

CUT FLOWER MIXTURE

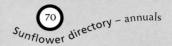

Evening Sun

HELIANTHUS ANNUUS

 PLANT HEIGHT:
6½–9 ft/2–2.7 m
IDEAL FOR:
focal point

The dramatic tall plants of 'Evening Sun' have unusually dark leaves and stalks. The large flowers (8-10 in/20-25 cm), come in a fantastic range of rich autumnal colors – mahogany-red, russet-bronze and gold. They have red-black centres surrounded by bi-colored petals consisting of an inner ring of deep maroon and an outer ring of rich red. Quite a few secondary blooms make it a must for sunflower lovers.

Floristan

HELIANTHUS ANNUUS

 PLANT HEIGHT:
3–4 ft/90 cm–1.2 m
IDEAL FOR:
border planting, flower arranging

The flowers of 'Floristan' have very unusual, yellow-tipped, red-brown petals. It is a branching sunflower and bears masses of flowers – a dream for the flower arranger. Besides being good for cutting, 'Floristan' looks stunning in a border.

Full Sun

HELIANTHUS ANNUUS

 PLANT HEIGHT:
5 ft/1.5 m
IDEAL FOR:
border planting, flower arranging

'Full Sun' has been specially bred to start flowering early and to continue flowering throughout the summer. It is an extremely vigoros F1 hybrid with deep golden-yellow blooms and thick, strong stems and dark green leaves. The large flowers (1 ft/30 cm) are unusual in that they naturally face upwards. Being pollen free, 'Full Sun' cannot shed, making it perfect for cutting.

FULL SUN

GIANT YELLOW

Giant Single

HELIANTHUS ANNUUS

PLANT HEIGHT:
6-10 ft/1.8-3 m
IDEAL FOR:
children

The 'Giant Single' produces enormous golden-yellow flowers surrounding a large, brown centre. It has a very long flowering period (July to September), so gives immense value for money. It is also easy to grow, which combined with its height makes it a winner with children. 'Giant Single' seeds are widely available.

Giant Yellow

HELIANTHUS ANNUUS

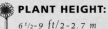

PLANT HEIGHT:
6¹/₂-9 ft/2-2.7 m
IDEAL FOR:
breaking records, screen

If you want to try and break some records, this is one of the best varieties to go for. Or try planting it as a screen or 'avenue' to line a pathway. The 'Giant Yellow's' immense height and giant, golden flowerheads are guaranteed to bewitch children and make it a good choice to grow with one of the bushier varieties as a living playhouse or den (see page 17).

Gloriosa Polyheaded

HELIANTHUS ANNUUS

PLANT HEIGHT:
6¹/₂-8 ft/2-2.4 m
IDEAL FOR:
flower arranging, focal point

This sunflower is remarkable for the immense number of branches it can produce – from 10 to an incredible 40. Its medium-sized flowers come in a wide range of vivid colors – from a bright yellow to a glorious sunny orange. Some flowers are even a mixture of orange and yellow with unusual red circles on each petal. It makes a wonderful focal point and is excellent for cutting.

GOLD AND SILVER

Happy Face

HELIANTHUS ANNUUS

 PLANT HEIGHT:
2-4 ft/60 cm-1.2 m
IDEAL FOR:
border planting, focal points

The name of this sunflower does not really convey how beautiful it is. The flowers are 5 in/13 cm wide with golden yellow petals and the most stunning disc, consisting of a halo of golden stamens surrounding a greeny-yellow centre. The leaves are an attractive deep green. A real beauty, and a must for all sunflower fans.

Henry Wilde

HELIANTHUS HYBRIDUS

 PLANT HEIGHT:
4-6 ft/1.2-1.8 m
IDEAL FOR:
flower arranging

'Henry Wilde' is one of the old varieties of sunflower and very gracious looking. Its striking flowers consist of soft orange-yellow petals surrounding a dark chocolate-colored centre. It is branched and bears a number of useful secondary blooms. Its warm hues look very good in flower arrangements.

Gold and Silver

 **PLANT HEIGHT:**   **HELIANTHUS ANNUUS**
5 ft/1.5 m
IDEAL FOR:
border planting, flower arranging

One of the newest varieties, 'Gold and Silver' has golden flowers, but what makes it really stand out from the crowd is its unusual and attractive silvery foliage. An excellent choice for garden borders and for flower arrangements, where its remarkable foliage can be fully appreciated. Looks stunning planted with hostas.

HENRY WILDE

Holiday

HELIANTHUS ANNUUS

PLANT HEIGHT:
4-5 ft/1.2-1.5 m
IDEAL FOR:
children, flower arranging

This is one of the classic sunflowers. It has multi-branching stems which can spread to as much as 4 ft/1.2 m, all bearing cheerful, open-faced flowers. These blooms (which are about 6 in/15 cm in diameter), have golden-yellow petals and dark brown centers. They are especially good for cutting, looking wonderful in a vase and lasting well in water.

Hopi Dye

HELIANTHUS ANNUUS

PLANT HEIGHT:
6 ft/1.8 m
IDEAL FOR:
border planting

As the name suggests, this variety was used by the North American Hopi tribe to make dye. This dye would have been used for anything from decorating pots and baskets to the body. They also used the seeds for food for themselves and their animals. Besides the main flowers (which are 5 in/13 cm), this variety also bears smaller side blooms. Flowers consist of yellow petals surrounding an unusual purple-green central disk. This purple color is echoed on the stalk, just underneath the leaves. It grows particularly well in cool, high areas (like its native habitat). May need staking.

Inca Jewels

HELIANTHUS ANNUUS

PLANT HEIGHT:
6 ft/1.8 m
IDEAL FOR:
flower arranging, informal hedge

This is a beautifully bred mix of 5 or more different floral types in delicious colors ranging from a creamy-yellow to a strong orange-yellow. Some flowers bear a distinctive halo of color, ranging from a rich maroon to a reddish-brown or copper, all around a stunning ochre-orange central disc. Strong, multi-branching stems will produce secondary blooms. Works wonderfully cut for flower arranging or as an informal hedge. Early flowering.

HOLIDAY (SEE PAGE 73)

INCREDIBLE

Incredible

HELIANTHUS ANNUUS

PLANT HEIGHT:
2 ft/60 cm
IDEAL FOR:
border planting, edging

'Incredible' has very large (10 in/ 25 cm), vivid yellow flower heads with an astonishing chocolate-colored seedhead, with a ring of bright yellow seeds in the centre. These are borne on strong dwarf stems, making it a stunning choice for the front of a border or to edge a path. It has a usefully long flowering period – from July through to September.

Israeli

HELIANTHUS ANNUUS

PLANT HEIGHT:
4-6 ft/1.2-1.8 m
IDEAL FOR:
crop

This is a sturdy, single-stemmed variety which bears one large (10-14 in/25-35 cm), bright orange flower. 'Israeli' is also particularly valuable for its delicious, large seeds. These are black and white and prove very popular with the birds, so net your plants well if you want to save any for yourself.

Italian White

HELIANTHUS DEBILIS

PLANT HEIGHT:
4–6 ft/1.2–1.8 m

IDEAL FOR:
ornamental hedge, border planting

The delicate colors of this exquisite sunflower are quite breathtaking. The medium-sized blooms range from a creamy-white to the palest-yellow, and all have deep brown-black centres, making a striking contrast. The 'Italian White' sunflower has a long flowering period and is also multi-branching, which makes it perfect for an ornamental hedge.

ITALIAN WHITE

Jumbo

HELIANTHUS ANNUUS

PLANT HEIGHT:
8 ft/2.4 m

IDEAL FOR:
crop

The giant (1 ft/30 cm and upwards), heads of this striking yellow sunflower produce very attractive, fat, black-and-white striped seeds. These can grow to an incredible 1 cm/½ in wide and are edible for humans. The large size of the seeds makes removing the shells easy.

Kid's Stuff

HELIANTHUS ANNUUS

PLANT HEIGHT:
2½ ft/75 cm

IDEAL FOR:
border planting, children, edging

Naturally, children will adore this perfectly proportioned little sunflower and their parents will love it for its contribution to the border, as it makes a stunning border or edging plant. It also bears a mass of golden flowers which reach a diameter of 10 in/26 cm.

Lemon Queen

HELIANTHUS ANNUUS

PLANT HEIGHT:
5–7 ft/1.5–2.1 m

IDEAL FOR:
screen

'Lemon Queen' is a free-flowering variety with beautiful, dark-centred, creamy-lemon flowers. The medium-sized blooms of 'Lemon Queen' come into flower mid-season and, if densely planted in a row, make a particularly effective screen, perfect for hiding eyesores.

LEMON QUEEN

MOONWALKER

Mammoth Russian (a.k.a. Mammoth Grey Stripe)

PLANT HEIGHT:
7-9 ft/2.1-2.7 m
IDEAL FOR:
breaking records, crop

HELIANTHUS ANNUUS

This sunflower is unusual in that it was bred in Russia and exported to the United States at the end of the last century. It is extremely easy to grow and has tremendous, large (10-12 in/25-30 cm), classic flowers with bright, open faces. The orange-yellow petals surround an orange disc, making it very attractive. Another bonus is that the thin-shelled, grey-white striped seeds are extremely good for eating, so after you've made it into the record books you can celebrate by baking a cake containing some of your winning plant.

Moonwalker and Moonbright

HELIANTHUS ANNUUS

 PLANT HEIGHT:
4-5 ft/1.2-1.5 m
IDEAL FOR:
border planting, flower arranging

'Moonwalker' is a branching sunflower, whose stems each hold 8-10 large flowers. These are made up of spectacular, acid-yellow petals surrounding a rich, dark brown central disc. Also look out for the similar 'Moonbright'. This grows to about the same height and has bright lemon-yellow petals with a dark brown disc. These are both striking sunflowers for the garden and are good for cutting.

Music Box Mixed

HELIANTHUS ANNUUS

 PLANT HEIGHT:
2-3 ft/60-90 cm
IDEAL FOR:
containers, flower arranging

'Music Box Mixed' is a bushy, compact, branching sunflower. It produces a good variety of unusual-colored blooms, from creamy-yellow to a rich, deep, flaming red, all with a very dark, almost black centre. Also available in bi-colored flowers. This variety is perfect for containers and cutting. The 4-5 in/10-12 cm flowers have a long season, blooming from July all the way through October.

Pacino

HELIANTHUS ANNUUS

PLANT HEIGHT:
45 cm/1 ½ ft
IDEAL FOR:
containers, edging

This dwarf plant produces numerous branches which all bear a mass of 10-13 cm/4-5 in flower heads with bright sunny yellow petals. This is a particularly valuable variety as it will thrive in containers as small as 10 cm/4 in. It is also extremely useful for edging a border or pathway.

Pastiche

HELIANTHUS ANNUUS

PLANT HEIGHT:
1.2-1.8 m/4-6 ft
IDEAL FOR:
border planting, flower arranging, screen

'Pastiche' produces flowers in a wonderful range of colors and combinations, from vivid yellows, through hot reds. The flowerheads' central discs also come in different colors – some being bright yellow and others rich red. It is long-lasting when cut and looks stupendous in a mixed border or as a screen. Plant in a circle to make a hideaway for little children (see page 17).

PASTICHE

Paul Bunyon

HELIANTHUS ANNUUS

PLANT HEIGHT:
15 ft/4.5 m
IDEAL FOR:
breaking records, crop, focal point

'Paul Bunyon' is a real monster with a huge yellow head (20 in/ 50 cm wide), to match its enormous height. Just a few of these, strategically planted, will draw gasps of admiration. Arrange them in a group to create a sunflower copse.

Peredovik

HELIANTHUS ANNUUS

PLANT HEIGHT:
5-6 ft/1.5-1.8 m
IDEAL FOR:
bird food, crop

This is a Russian variety bred for commercial use to yield oil and seed for birdfood mixes. It has a few side branches and produces pure black, elongated seeds. If you want to attract a wide variety of beautiful birds then give them a ready-made feast by cutting off the seedheads when they are ripe and hanging them up around the garden from trees or posts. You will be staggered at how many species you will attract. Other varieties much loved by the birds are 'Sundak' and 'Arrowhead'. For seeds for humans to snack on, grow 'Jumbo' (8 ft/2.4 m high with 1 ft/30 cm heads) which produces very large black and white striped seeds.

Prado Red and Prado Yellow

HELIANTHUS ANNUUS

PLANT HEIGHT:
4-5 ft/1.2-1.5 m
IDEAL FOR:
border planting, flower arranging

'Prado Red' and 'Prado Yellow' (sometimes known as 'Prado Gold'), are virtually pollen-less, multi-flowered (F1 hybrid) plants producing beautiful blooms. 'Prado Red' comes in a rich burgundy red, while 'Prado Yellow' is a bright, clear yellow. If you are keen on flower arranging, choose 'Prado Yellow' which, unlike 'Prado Red', lasts well in a vase. If you pinch out the first buds you will encourage development of perfect stems with flawless flowers.

PRADO YELLOW   **PRADO RED**

Red Sun

HELIANTHUS ANNUUS

 PLANT HEIGHT:
6 ft/1.8 m
IDEAL FOR:
focal point

A lovely variety which has almost autumnal coloring. The blooms are a deep red and have very unusual brown centres which are ringed with a faint halo of yellow. These pretty flowers are medium-sized, yet are so attractive that they are quite able to hold their own if planted as focal points.

Russian Giant

HELIANTHUS ANNUUS

 PLANT HEIGHT:
8-10 ft/2.4-3 m
IDEAL FOR:
breaking records

As its name suggests, this sunflower is one of the giants. It is one of the tallest sunflowers available and is guaranteed to make you feel like Gulliver in the land of Brobdingnag when you stand beside it. Its yellow-petalled flowers have unusual greeny-brown central discs, making them very eye-catching.

RUSSIAN GIANT

Russian Mammoth (Diane's Strain)

PLANT HEIGHT: HELIANTHUS ANNUUS
10 ft/3 m
IDEAL FOR:
breaking records, focal point, screen

Aim to break the record for flower diameter with this variety, as its flowers can grow as wide as 20 in/50 cm. Obviously this makes it excellent as a focal point or to screen off any eyesore. If you are aiming to grow especially large blooms then give the sunflowers a bit of space, planting them about 3-5 ft/90 cm-1.5 m apart.

Silver Leaf Sunflower

HELIANTHUS ARGOPHYLLUS

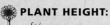

PLANT HEIGHT:
6 ft/1.8 m
IDEAL FOR:
flower arranging

The flowers of this variety are quite small, but what they lack in size they make up for in brightness. The blooms consist of vivid, sunshine-yellow petals around brownish-purple centers. In addition to its bright hue, this variety is worth seeking out for its unusual, grey, silky leaves which look wonderful and last indefinitely when dried.

Sonja

HELIANTHUS ANNUUS

PLANT HEIGHT:
3 ft/90 cm
IDEAL FOR:
flower arranging, focal point

This upright sunflower has won awards, and rightly so, for it produces at least eight strong side branches all topped by stunning 4 in/10 cm tangerine-orange flowers with dark centers. It is extremely good for cutting as it is very long lasting in water, and its dramatic looks are guaranteed to turn heads.

Southern Lights

HELIANTHUS ANNUUS

PLANT HEIGHT:
5 ft/1.5 m
IDEAL FOR:
bird food, border planting, children

A variety introduced in the early nineties which will light up any border with its rich, jewel-like colors. The medium-sized ray flowers come in an acid-lemon hue which blends to gold, rich chocolate-brown and opulent burgundy. The black central discs serve to accentuate the petal colors. 'Southern Lights' blooms for a glorious 60 days, bearing slightly smaller secondary blooms once the first are over. May need to be staked. Birds adore it.

SONJA

Stella

HELIANTHUS ANNUUS

PLANT HEIGHT:
4 ft/1.2 m
IDEAL FOR:
border planting

This is one of the few original sunflower varieties, and is mentioned in documents as early as the mid-nineteenth century. The very fact that 'Stella' is still so popular today says a lot for its quality. It is a multi-branching sunflower, with each of the numerous stems proudly bearing a few classic sunflowers. 'Stella' has rich orange-yellow flowers with dark central discs.

Summer Days Cut Flower Mixed

HELIANTHUS ANNUUS

PLANT HEIGHT:
5 ft/1.5 m
IDEAL FOR:
border planting, flower arranging

Another of the new breeds with an attractive branching habit. This variety is really excellent for cutting as it is so long-lasting in water. There are a good selection of colors, ranging from a sunny, summer yellow to a deep, autumnal bronze.

SUNBEAM

Sunbeam

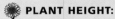 **PLANT HEIGHT:**
5 ft/1.5 m
IDEAL FOR:
focal point

HELIANTHUS ANNUUS

'Sunbeam', an F1 hybrid, is early-flowering and bears very unusual flowers. They are of medium size with petals a fairly typical sunflower yellow, but how they differ from their relations is in the color of the central disc. For 'Sunbeam' has a very striking bright green center. This makes it excellent as a focal point for the garden.

Sunbright

HELIANTHUS ANNUUS

PLANT HEIGHT:
5-6 ft/1.5-1.8 m
IDEAL FOR:
border planting

One of the classic sunflowers, being tall with 6 in/15 cm flowers consisting of sunny golden petals surrounding a dark brown center. Its stature makes it a perfect choice for the back of the border or, in a traditional cottage garden, for mingling with the hollyhocks beside an entrance or along a path.

Sunburst Mixed

HELIANTHUS ANNUUS

PLANT HEIGHT:
4 ft/1.2 m
IDEAL FOR:
border planting

A lovely mixture producing a wide range . of beautifully colored 4 in/10 cm blooms – gold, light primrose, bronze and rich crimson – borne on tough, branching stems. Some of the flowers are bi-colored, so are especially pretty.

SUNBRIGHT

Sundak

PLANT HEIGHT:
6 ft / 1.8 m
IDEAL FOR:
bird food

HELIANTHUS ANNUUS

This is grown commercially for seed, however, there is no reason it cannot be grown in the garden. It is a firm favorite with birds, so remember to harvest the seeds to give the neighborhood birds a tasty treat. Grow this with other varieties and it will give them some protection from being eaten by birds. A mid-yellow shade.

Sunrich Series

(a.k.a. Oranges and Lemons)

HELIANTHUS ANNUUS

PLANT HEIGHT:
4 - 5 ft / 1.2 - 1.5 m
IDEAL FOR:
flower arranging

'Sunrich Series' are single-stemmed F1 hybrid sunflowers. The medium-sized, pollenless blooms are quite beautiful, being densely-petalled. There are two basic color choices – 'Sunrich Orange', which has stunning golden-orange petals around a striking black center, and 'Sunrich Lemon', which also has a black central disc, although the petals are a wonderful lemony-yellow. They make lovely cut flowers, being very long lasting when cut, as well as looking fabulous in the garden.

Sunrise

HELIANTHUS ANNUUS

PLANT HEIGHT:
5 ft / 1.5 m
IDEAL FOR:
border planting, cutting

The large (6 in/15 cm) lemony-yellow flowers on this base-branching sunflower will brighten up any border with their cheerful countenance. They are also very long-lasting when cut so are a good choice for flower arrangers.

Sun Series

HELIANTHUS ANNUUS

PLANT HEIGHT:
5 - 6 ft / 1.5 - 1.8 m
IDEAL FOR:
flower arranging

Another F1 hybrid, bred to be vigoros. 'Sun Series' is single-stemmed and produces pollenless 4-6 in /10-15 cm golden blooms which are so perfect as to be virtually flawless. Unusually, it copes well with low temperatures and short days and is an excellent choice for cutting. Try growing it in a heated greenhouse in the winter.

Sunseed

HELIANTHUS ANNUUS

PLANT HEIGHT:
4 - 5 ft / 1.2 - 1.5 m
IDEAL FOR:
bird food, border planting, pet food

This F1 hybrid matures very quickly and the enormous heads (12-16 in/30-40 cm), produce a good quantity of seeds which are very rich in oil and adored by birds and pets. The useful height of this variety and its big head make it an excellent choice for a border, where its attractive vivid yellow petals surrounding an outer circle of bright orange stamens look wonderfully pretty.

Sunset

HELIANTHUS ANNUUS

PLANT HEIGHT:
3 ft/90 cm

IDEAL FOR:
border planting, flower arranging

The 6 in/15 cm flowers of this lovely sunflower have warm mahogany petals tipped with a touch of gold. The plants are base-branching and produce an abundance of blooms which look simply stunning in arrangements. Plant in a clump in front of 'Sunrise' for a show-stopping duet.

Sunshine

HELIANTHUS ANNUUS

PLANT HEIGHT:
6 1/2-8 ft/2-2.4 m

IDEAL FOR:
focal point

Another of the brand new varieties, 'Sunshine' has show-stopping blooms (4-8 in/ 10-20 cm). This sunflower has multi-branching stems all bearing cheerful, bright orange-gold, medium-sized flowers which will provide a welcome splash of color to any garden.

Sunspot

HELIANTHUS ANNUUS

PLANT HEIGHT:
1 1/2-2 ft/45-60 cm

IDEAL FOR:
children, containers

'Sunspot' is an unusual sunflower in that it is dwarf yet can bear extremely big blooms – they can grow to 8-10 in/20-25 cm. These golden flowers, with their large cheerful heads, look stunning in containers. Being moveable, you could vary their position, grouping them on the terrace when you eat out, or moving them to a darker spot if the garden needs livening up.

SUNSPOT

Sun 891

HELIANTHUS ANNUUS

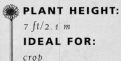 **PLANT HEIGHT:**
7 ft/2.1 m
IDEAL FOR:
crop

Despite its unromantic name, the F1 hybrid variety 'Sun 891' is a natural choice for anyone wanting to grow sunflowers as a crop. It is early-ripening and produces really delicious seeds on its large (8-12 in/20-30 cm) heads. Needless to say, the birds also find these seeds delicious, so to be sure of a good crop it is best to net the sunflowers well.

Taiyo

HELIANTHUS ANNUUS

PLANT HEIGHT:
4-10 ft/1.2-3 m
IDEAL FOR:
border planting, flower arrangements

'Taiyo' comes from Japan originally, where its name, appropriately, means 'sun'. These are stunning, large, single-stemmed plants which bear huge (8-12 in/20-30 cm), golden-yellow flowers with deep brown centers. They have shiny petals which seem to accentuate their brightness. 'Taiyo' is very fast-growing as well as being long-lasting when cut, which makes it ideal for large, theatrical arrangements.

Tangina

HELIANTHUS ANNUUS

PLANT HEIGHT:
3 ft/90 cm
IDEAL FOR:
border planting

This new branching sunflower bears 4 in/10 cm blooms with orange petals and dark brown centers. They look stupendous grown on their own and planted beside the more usual yellow varieties make a nice contrast. They will also make a splash if planted in a large clump.

Tall Single

HELIANTHUS ANNUUS

PLANT HEIGHT:
6-8 ft/1.8-2.4 m
IDEAL FOR:
bird food, focal point

This variety is notable for the giant flower heads which produce masses of seeds. Although it is excellent as a focal point due to its large blooms, it is worth growing simply for the seeds, which dried and stored will produce next year's display. It flowers from July to September. There is also a 'Tall Single Mixed' variety.

Tarahumara White Shelled

HELIANTHUS ANNUUS

PLANT HEIGHT:
7 ft/2.1 m
IDEAL FOR:
focal point, crop

A rare but easily grown variety, the 'Tarahumara White Shelled' makes a spectacular focal point. The towering stems of this traditional sunflower bear one large, deep-gold flower. This beautiful bloom yields quite delicious, white-shelled seeds.

FIELD OF SUNSPOTS

TITAN

Tiger's Eye Mix

HELIANTHUS ANNUUS

PLANT HEIGHT:
6 1/2–8 ft/2–2.4 m
IDEAL FOR:
border planting

'Tiger's Eye Mix' is a brand new variety with medium-sized flowers on multi-branching stems. The petals and discs come in a wide variety of striking colors, ranging from a hot yellow to a deep gold and rich coppery-bronze. The flowers are notable for their striking central discs, which are unusually large and curiously fluffy.

Titan

HELIANTHUS ANNUUS

PLANT HEIGHT:
12 ft/3.6 m
IDEAL FOR:
focal point

Another giant which makes a stunning focal point. The astonishingly large flowerheads of 'Titan' (2 ft/60 cm), are sure to turn heads. Planted at the back of a border it looks just tremendous, while you can grow your own summertime guard of honor if you plant a couple of Titans on either side of a door or gateway.

VALENTINE

Valentine

PLANT HEIGHT: HELIANTHUS ANNUUS
5 ft/1.5 m
IDEAL FOR:
flower arranging

This semi-dwarf variety produces a host of branches from its base, all bearing masses of lovely, lemony-yellow blooms with near-black centers from July to October. The nicely angled stems are excellent for cutting as the flowers face outwards, which means they display their pretty faces to advantage. 'Valentine' bears lots of large primary flowers, with a quantity of good-sized secondary ones too, all of which are very long-lasting in water. It is best to cut the flowers just as they start to come into bud.

VANILLA ICE

Vanilla Ice

HELIANTHUS DEBILIS

 PLANT HEIGHT:
5 ft/1.5 m
IDEAL FOR:
flower arranging, focal point

This is one of the most elegant sunflowers. The graceful, large, creamy-yellow blooms with their rich, chocolate-colored centers are borne on strong, branching stems and look quite stupendous as a focal point in a border. Their striking good looks will not fail to draw the eye in the garden, while in the house they are grand enough to grace the smartest party.

Velvet Queen

HELIANTHUS ANNUUS

PLANT HEIGHT:
5-6 ft/1.5-1.8 m
IDEAL FOR:
flower arranging, focal point

This variety boasts the darkest blooms of any sunflower. They come in a wonderful range of deep colors, from rich chestnut red, through to burgundy and bronze. All the flowers (5 in/ 13 cm), have striking dark centers, and some even possess a lovely dark 'halo' at the innermost edge of the petals. The sturdy stems are branching. 'Velvet Queen' flowers in summer.

VELVET QUEEN

Velvet Tapestries

PLANT HEIGHT: **HELIANTHUS ANNUUS**
5 ft/1.5 m
IDEAL FOR:
border planting, flower arranging

Look out for 'Velvet Tapestries', which bears 6 in/15 cm flowers in glowing shades of gold, red and beige – some even being bi-colored. It is excellent for flower arrangements and has a silky look similar to the petals of 'Velvet Queen', which cry out to be stroked.

Double blooms

Bred to be fluffy, the double bloom varieties of sunflowers look more like chrysanthemums than their single bloom counterparts.

Chrysanthemum -flowered series

HELIANTHUS ANNUUS

 PLANT HEIGHT:
5 ft/1.5 m
IDEAL FOR:
screen

This variety has orange-yellow double flowers (6 in/15 cm), borne in mid-summer above large, mid-green leaves with serrated edges. It is fast growing; therefore makes an ideal screen.

Giant Sungold

 PLANT HEIGHT:
5-6 ft/1.5-1.8 m
IDEAL FOR:
focal point, screen, flower arranging

HELIANTHUS ANNUUS

This sunflower bears large (8 in/20 cm), vivid golden-yellow fully double flowers. These stand out particularly well in the garden as they bloom in late summer when other bright flowers are fading away. They are also good for cutting, and for a really fabulous effect, arrange them in a bright blue or emerald green vase. This will intensify their color, making a truly dazzling display.

Lion's Mane

HELIANTHUS ANNUUS

PLANT HEIGHT:
6 ft/1.8 m
IDEAL FOR:
border planting

The flowers of 'Lion's Mane' are quite similar to those of 'Teddy Bear' (vivid orange with fully double petals). However, it is much taller, growing to 6 ft/ 1.8 m. 'Lion's Mane' is a strong single-stemmed variety and the lovely soft-looking flowers look somewhat like pom-poms.

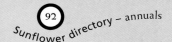

ORANGE SUN

Orange Sun

HELIANTHUS ANNUUS

 PLANT HEIGHT:
5-6 ft/1.5-1.8 m
IDEAL FOR:
containers, borders, flower arranging

As the name suggests, 'Orange Sun' is a wonderful, vibrant orange color. The flowers are pom-pom shaped, 6 in/15 cm in diameter. Unusually, they develop to reveal bright green centers. Widely available, and happy in containers or in the open garden.

GIANT SUNGOLD

Prairie Sunflower

HELIANTHUS PETIOLARIS

PLANT HEIGHT:
6 ft/1.8 m
IDEAL FOR:
focal point

Create your own miniature prairie with this lovely sunflower. It produces glorious bright yellow flowers with rich brown centers in late summer to early autumn. An unusual feature is its strange triangular leaves, quite unlike those of any other sunflower. It is more at home in the New World than the Old; however, with care and attention, it will grow quite happily in Europe.

Sungold Double

HELIANTHUS ANNUUS

PLANT HEIGHT:
4-5 ft/1.2-1.5 m
IDEAL FOR:
border planting

The wonderful, golden, mop-top flowers of the 'Sungold Double' sit on top of its tall stems like beacons. This is a perfect variety for the back of a border as its height will ensure it does not get lost.

SUNGOLD DOUBLE

TEDDY BEAR

Teddy Bear
(a.k.a. Golden Globe)

HELIANTHUS ANNUUS

 PLANT HEIGHT:
1-2 ft/30-60 cm
IDEAL FOR:
containers, flower arranging, children, border planting

This popular variety is as cuddly as its name implies. It is a dwarf, only reaching a couple of feet when fully grown, and bears a fluffy mass of fully double, deep-yellow blooms about 6 in/15 cm in diameter. 'Teddy Bear' looks wonderful planted in containers and will light up the house if cut and placed in a vase.

Tohoku Yae

HELIANTHUS ANNUUS

 PLANT HEIGHT:
4-5 ft/1.2-1.5 m
IDEAL FOR:
focal point

This brand new variety is quite unlike any other sunflower. The single, upright, fully-double, orange-yellow blooms (5-7 in/ 13-18 cm), are surrounded by a single band, or ruff, of golden petals. The dark green foliage contrasts dramatically with the mop-top flowers. This is a real show-stopper in any garden.

Perennials

Perennials come into bloom in the mid summer and early autumn – a time when many herbaceous plants are dying off and the garden is starting to look somewhat drab. There are more than 40 varieties of perennial sunflower, so there is bound to be a variety to suit you. Like annuals, perennial sunflowers come in single and double forms.

Single blooms

An essential ingredient for any serious gardener, the single perennials are bushier than annuals therefore perfect to edge a path or border.

CAPENOCH STAR

Capenoch Star

PLANT HEIGHT:
4-6 ft/1.2-1.8 m
IDEAL FOR:
border planting

**HELIANTHUS DECAPETALUS
(SYN. H. X MULTIFLORUS)**

'Capenoch Star' is a lovely branching variety bearing lemony-yellow 3 in/7.5 cm blooms above lance-shaped mid-green leaves. It flowers throughout the summer, from July/August through September. It will sit happily at the back of a border, or could even be grown in a bed on its own for maximum impact.

Giant Sunflower

HELIANTHUS GIGANTEUS

PLANT HEIGHT:
9-12 ft/2.7-3.6 m
IDEAL FOR:
focal point

Not surprisingly, given its name, the 'Giant Sunflower' is very tall. But it is not just worthy of mention for its height, as it also produces very pretty light yellow flowers which bloom from August to October.

Helianthus x multiflorus

**HELIANTHUS X
MULTIFLORUS**

PLANT HEIGHT:
5 ft/1.5 m
IDEAL FOR:
border planting

The large, golden-yellow blooms of this lovely variety are borne in late summer and early autumn. It will need staking and has a tendency to be invasive, so keep a careful watch on it to keep it under control. This is a very bushy variety, and if planted closely together makes an extremely effective bushy screen or informal hedge.

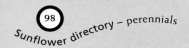

Helianthus nuttallii

PLANT HEIGHT:
5-10 ft/1.5-3 m
IDEAL FOR:
border planting, flower arranging

HELIANTHUS NUTTALLII

This perennial sunflower is very hardy, forming clumps which will produce mainly single stems. Each of these stems carries golden-yellow blooms about 3-4 in/8-10 cm in diameter. The flowers appear in the late summer through to autumn. *Helianthus nuttallii* looks fabulous in the garden but is also ideal for cutting.

Maximilian

PLANT HEIGHT:
6-8 ft/1.8-2.4 m
IDEAL FOR:
border planting, flower arranging

HELIANTHUS MAXIMILIANII

An easy-to-grow sunflower, 'Maximilian' is guaranteed to draw the eye with its lofty stature, lanced leaves and masses of medium-sized (2-3 in/ 5-8 cm), deep yellow flowers. It is long-flowering – from August to first frosts – and helpfully renews itself from the base every year. A large group will look impressive in a border and it is a good choice if you want a variety for cutting.

Naked Sunflower

PLANT HEIGHT:
2-3 ft/60-90 cm
IDEAL FOR:
border planting, crop

HELIANTHUS OCCIDENTALIS

The lovely yellow blooms of the 'Naked Sunflower' are borne from August through September. If growing as a crop, be sure to net the flowers otherwise the birds will soon devour all the seeds.

Saw-tooth Sunflower

HELIANTHUS GROSSESERRATUS

PLANT HEIGHT:
2-8 ft/60 cm-2.4 m
IDEAL FOR:
border planting, birds

While many of the perennial sunflowers can be invasive, the North American 'Saw-Tooth Sunflower' is one of the most aggressive. Unusually, it is happiest in wet areas, as long as it has full sun. It bears yellow blooms for a long flowering period, from July to October. It looks tremendous at the back of a border and will attract flocks of birds in the autumn.

Swamp Sunflower

HELIANTHUS ANGUSTIFOLIUS

PLANT HEIGHT:
6-7 ft/1.8-2.1 m
IDEAL FOR:
border planting

Another variety which is probably happiest in North America, the 'Swamp Sunflower' has unusual, thin, grass-like leaves topped by yellow flowers with purplish central discs. It is in bloom from August to October.

Thin-leaf Sunflower

HELIANTHUS DECAPETALUS

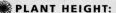

PLANT HEIGHT:
3-5 ft/90 cm-1.5 m
IDEAL FOR:
border planting

One of the shorter varieties, the 'Thin-Leaf Sunflower' is in bloom from mid- to late-summer. Its flowers are yellow and sit above strangely toothed leaves. The main feature of this variety is its lovely smooth stems; they cry out to be stroked, so plant them beside a path or somewhere accessible.

Willow-leaved sunflower

HELIANTHUS SALICIFOLIUS (SYN. H. ORGYALIS)

PLANT HEIGHT:
7-9 ft/2.1-2.7 m
IDEAL FOR:
border planting

This is an early autumn flowering variety producing close-set strong stems with drooping long, mid-green, elongated leaves from which the variety gets its name. The small golden-yellow flowers (they only reach about 2 in/5 cm across), are borne on strong branching stems, and form attractive sprays of color.

Woodland Sunflower

HELIANTHUS STRUMOSUS (SYN. H. DIVARICATUS)

PLANT HEIGHT:
4-6 ft/1.2-1.8 m
IDEAL FOR:
border planting, birds

An unusual sunflower which, as its name suggests, is happiest in sites with filtered, rather than full, sunlight, making it perfect for tricky, slightly shaded spots. It bears large yellow flowers from August through October and loves a well-drained soil – it can even cope with sand – so is good for any problem dry areas. It can be invasive.

MAXIMILIAN

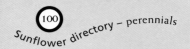

Double and semi-double blooms

The smallest of the sunflower groups, the double perennials still have an important role to play, especially when creating stunning border displays.

Flore-Pleno

PLANT HEIGHT:
6 ft/1.8 m
IDEAL FOR:
focal point

HELIANTHUS DECAPETALUS (SYN. H. X MULTIFLORUS)

A stately sunflower which produces beautiful double, clear yellow flowers (3 in/7.5 cm) as lovely as its name. The elegance of the flowers is accentuated by the leaves, which are mid-green and have an unexpectedly rough texture. 'Flore-Pleno' blooms from mid-summer.

Loddon Gold

HELIANTHUS DECAPETALUS (SYN. H. X MULTIFLORUS)

PLANT HEIGHT:
5 ft/1.5 m
IDEAL FOR:
border planting, edging

This is one of the most popular perennial sunflowers, partly because it is one of the bushiest varieties. This makes it ideal for edging a path or filling out the center of a border. It bears fully double, golden-yellow 3 in/ 7.5 cm flowers in late summer, which will light up your garden.

FLORE-PLENO

LODDON GOLD

Monarch

HELIANTHUS ATRORUBENS

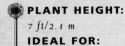

PLANT HEIGHT:
7 ft/2.1 m
IDEAL FOR:
border planting

A grandly titled sunflower which bears suitably regal semi-double golden blooms in the late summer. 'Monarch' has branching stems and mid-green, lance-shaped leaves. Best grown in good-sized clumps.

Showy Sunflower

HELIANTHUS X LAETIFLORUS

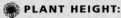

PLANT HEIGHT:
4-8 ft/1.2-2.4 m
IDEAL FOR:
border planting, flower arranging

This is a wonderfully easy-to-grow variety which is excellent for cutting. This tall sunflower bears semi-double, sunny yellow 4 in/10 cm flowers with a purplish center and unusual lance-shaped leaves. It flowers usefully late – from late summer well into early autumn – just as the late summer stars are starting to die back, so is invaluable for lifting a drab border.

MONARCH

Soleil D'or

HELIANTHUS DECAPETALUS (SYN. H. X MULTIFLORUS)

PLANT HEIGHT:
6 ft/1.8 m
IDEAL FOR:
border planting

A pretty, semi-double variety bearing smallish (3 in/7.5 cm), pale- to golden-yellow flowers from mid-summer onwards. Its mid-green leaves are sharply toothed and rough to the touch. Plant 'Soleil D'or' in a mass to get the best effect, from the relatively small flowers.

SOLEIL D'OR

Jerusalem Artichoke

HELIANTHUS TUBEROSUS

PLANT HEIGHT:
6½-10 ft/2-3 m
IDEAL FOR:
crop, shelter and screen

The strangest member of the sunflower family, Jerusalem artichokes are perennials with attractive foliage, mainly cultivated for their delicious edible tubers. You can grow jerusalem artichokes from their tubers.

The tubers do best planted in the spring, and although they can be tricky to get started, once established they grow with gusto – in fact given half a chance they will soon take over the vegetable garden. You will need to keep them firmly in check, preferably in a bed of their own, or else dig up the plants after harvesting and start again each year.

Sunflower uses

Bird food

African Sunset (*Helianthus annuus*)
Autumn Beauty (*Helianthus annuus*)
Aztec Gold (*Helianthus annuus*)
Saw-tooth Sunflower (*Helianthus grosseserratus*)
Sunseed (*Helianthus annuus*)
Woodland Sunflower (*Helianthus strumosus*
    (*syn. H. divaricatus*))

Border planting

African Sunset (*Helianthus annuus*)
Capenoch Star (*Helianthus decapetalus*
    (*syn. H. x multiflorus*))
Color Fashion Mix (*Helianthus annuus*)
Common Sunflower (*Helianthus annuus*)
Discovery Mix (*Helianthus annuus*)
Floristan (*Helianthus annuus*)
Full Sun (*Helianthus annuus*)
Gold and Silver (*Helianthus annuus*)
Happy Face (*Helianthus annuus*)
Helianthus nuttallii (*Helianthus nuttallii*)
Hopi Dye (*Helianthus annuus*)
Incredible (*Helianthus annuus*)
Italian White (*Helianthus debilis*)
Kid's Stuff (*Helianthus annuus*)
Lion's Mane (*Helianthus annuus*)
Loddon Gold (*Helianthus decapetalus*
    (*syn. H. x multiflorus*))
Monarch (*Helianthus atrorubens*)
Moonwalker (*Helianthus annuus*)
Naked Sunflower (*Helianthus occidentalis*)
Pastiche (*Helianthus annuus*)
Prado Red (*Helianthus annuus*)
Prado Yellow (*Helianthus annuus*)
Saw-tooth Sunflower (*Helianthus grosseserratus*)
Showy Sunflower (*Helianthus x laetiflorus*)
Soleil D'or (*Helianthus decapetalus (syn. H. x multiflorus)*)
Southern Lights (*Helianthus annuus*)
Stella (*Helianthus annuus*)
Summer Days Cut Flower Mixed (*Helianthus annuus*)

Sunbright (*Helianthus annuus*)
Sunburst Mixed (*Helianthus annuus*)
Sungold Double (*Helianthus annuus*)
Sunrise (*Helianthus annuus*)
Sunset (*Helianthus annuus*)
Swamp Sunflower (*Helianthus angustifolius*)
Taiyo (*Helianthus annuus*)
Tangina (*Helianthus annuus*)
Thin-leaf Sunflower (*Helianthus decapetalus*)
Tiger's Eye Mix (*Helianthus annuus*)
Willow-leaved sunflower (*H. salicifolius (syn. H. orgyalis)*)
Woodland Sunflower (*H. strumosus (syn. H. divaricatus)*)

Breaking records

Giant Yellow (*Helianthus annuus*)
Mammoth Russian (a.k.a. Mammoth Grey Stripe)
    (*Helianthus annuus*)
Paul Bunyon (*Helianthus annuus*)
Russian Giant (*Helianthus annuus*)
Russian Mammoth (Diane's Strain) (*Helianthus annuus*)

Children

Giant Single (*Helianthus annuus*)
Kid Stuff (sic) (*Helianthus annuus*)
Teddy Bear (a.k.a. Golden Globe) (*Helianthus annuus*)

Containers

Big Smile (*Helianthus annuus*)
Music Box Mixed (*Helianthus annuus*)
Pacino (*Helianthus annuus*)
Sunspot (*Helianthus annuus*)
Teddy Bear (a.k.a. Golden Globe) (*Helianthus annuus*)

Crop

Aztec Gold (*Helianthus annuus*)
Common Sunflower (*Helianthus annuus*)

Israeli (*Helianthus annuus*)
Jerusalem artichoke (*Helianthus tuberosus*)
Jumbo (*Helianthus annuus*)
Naked Sunflower (*Helianthus occidentalis*)
Peredovik (*Helianthus annuus*)
Sun 891 (*Helianthus annuus*)

Edging

Incredible (*Helianthus annuus*)
Kid's Stuff (*Helianthus annuus*)
Loddon Gold (*Helianthus decapetalus*
  (*syn. H. x multiflorus*))
Pacino (*Helianthus annuus*)

Flower arranging
(FRESH OR DRIED)

African Sunset (*Helianthus annuus*)
Autumn Beauty (*Helianthus annuus*)
Chianti Hybrid (*Helianthus annuus*)
Color Fashion Mix (*Helianthus annuus*)
Cucumber-leaf Sunflower (*Helianthus debilis*)
Cut Flower Mixture (*Helianthus annuus*)
Endurance (*Helianthus argophyllus* x *annuus*)
Floristan (*Helianthus annuus*)
Full Sun (*Helianthus annuus*)
Giant Sungold (*Helianthus annuus*)
Gloriosa Polyheaded (*Helianthus annuus*)
Gold and Silver (*Helianthus annuus*)
Helianthus nuttallii (*Helianthus nuttallii*)
Henry Wilde (*Helianthus hybridus*)
Holiday (*Helianthus annuus*)
Inca Jewels (*Helianthus annuus*)
Maximilian (*Helianthus maximilianii*)
Moonwalker (*Helianthus annuus*)
Music Box Mixed (*Helianthus annuus*)
Pastiche (*Helianthus annuus*)
Prado Red (*Helianthus annuus*)
Prado Yellow (*Helianthus annuus*)
Showy Sunflower (*Helianthus laetiflorus*)
Silver Leaf Sunflower (*Helianthus argophyllus*)
Sonja (*Helianthus annuus*)
Summer Days Cut Flower Mixed (*Helianthus annuus*)
Sunrich Series (*Helianthus annuus*)
Sunrise (*Helianthus annuus*)
Sun Series (*Helianthus annuus*)
Sunset (*Helianthus annuus*)
Taiyo (*Helianthus annuus*)
Teddy Bear (a.k.a. Golden Globe) (*Helianthus annuus*)

Tohoku Yae (*Helianthus annuus*)
Valentine (*Helianthus annuus*)
Vanilla Ice (*Helianthus debilis*)
Velvet Queen (*Helianthus annuus*)
Velvet Tapestries (*Helianthus annuus*)

Focal point

Aztec Gold (*Helianthus annuus*)
Chianti Hybrid (*Helianthus annuus*)
Common Sunflower (*Helianthus annuus*)
Evening Sun (*Helianthus annuus*)
Flore-Pleno (*Helianthus decapetalus* (*syn. H. x multiflorus*))
Giant Sunflower (*Helianthus giganteus*)
Giant Sungold (*Helianthus annuus*)
Gloriosa Polyheaded (*Helianthus annuus*)
Happy Face (*Helianthus annuus*)
Paul Bunyon (*Helianthus annuus*)
Prairie Sunflower (*Helianthus petiolaris*)
Red Sun (*Helianthus annuus*)
Russian Mammoth (Diane's Strain) (*Helianthus annuus*)
Sonja (*Helianthus annuus*)
Sunbeam (*Helianthus annuus*)
Sunshine (*Helianthus annuus*)
Tarahumara White Shelled (*Helianthus annuus*)
Titan (*Helianthus annuus*)
Vanilla Ice (*Helianthus debilis*)
Velvet Queen (*Helianthus annuus*)

Hedge

Inca Jewels (*Helianthus annuus*)
Italian White (*Helianthus annuus*)

Screen

Autumn Beauty (*Helianthus annuus*)
Aztec Gold (*Helianthus annuus*)
Chrysanthemum-flowered series (*Helianthus annuus*)
Color Fashion Mix (*Helianthus annuus*)
Cucumber-leaf Sunflower (*Helianthus debilis*)
Giant Sungold (*Helianthus annuus*)
Jerusalem artichoke (*Helianthus tuberosus*)
Lemon Queen (*Helianthus annuus*)
Pastiche (*Helianthus annuus*)
Russian Mammoth (Diane's Strain) (*Helianthus annuus*)

Sunflower color guide

Bronze

Autumn Beauty (*Helianthus annuus*)
Evening Sun (*Helianthus annuus*)

Gold

Autumn Beauty (*Helianthus annuus*)
Aztec Gold (*Helianthus annuus*)
Evening Sun (*Helianthus annuus*)
Monarch (*Helianthus atrorubens*)
Soleil D'or (*Helianthus decapetalus* (syn. *H.* x *multiflorus*))
Tarahumara White Shelled (*Helianthus annuus*)
Velvet Tapestries (*Helianthus annuus*)

Lemon

Autumn Beauty (*Helianthus annuus*)
Capenoch Star (*Helianthus decapetalus*
   (syn. *H.* x *multiflorus*)
Lemon Queen (*Helianthus annuus*)
Sunrich Lemon (*Helianthus annuus*)
Sunrise (*Helianthus annuus*)
Valentine (*Helianthus annuus*)
Velvet Tapestries (*Helianthus annuus*)

Multi-colored

African Sunset (*Helianthus annuus*)
Color Fashion Mix (*Helianthus annuus*)
Cut Flower Mixture (*Helianthus annuus*)
Discovery Mix (*Helianthus annuus*)
Floristan (*Helianthus annuus*)
Inca Jewels (*Helianthus annuus*)
Music Box Mixed (*Helianthus annuus*)
Pastiche (*Helianthus annuus*)
Southern Lights (*Helianthus annuus*)
Summer Days Cut Flower Mixed (*Helianthus annuus*)
Sunburst Mixed (*Helianthus annuus*)
Tiger's Eye Mix (*Helianthus annuus*)
Velvet Tapestries (*Helianthus annuus*)

Orange

Gloriosa Polyheaded (*Helianthus annuus*)
Israeli (*Helianthus annuus*)
Lion's Mane (*Helianthus annuus*)
Mammoth Russian (*Helianthus annuus*)
Sonja (*Helianthus annuus*)
Sungold double (*Helianthus annuus*)
Sunrich Orange (*Helianthus annuus*)
Sunshine (*Helianthus annuus*)
Tangina (*Helianthus annuus*)

Red

Autumn Beauty (*Helianthus annuus*)
Chianti Hybrid (*Helianthus annuus*)
Evening Sun (*Helianthus annuus*)
Prado Red (*Helianthus annuus*)
Red Sun (*Helianthus annuus*)
Sunset (*Helianthus annuus*)
Velvet Queen (*Helianthus annuus*)

White

Italian White (*Helianthus debilis*)
Vanilla Ice (*Helianthus debilis*)

Yellow

Big Smile (*Helianthus annuus*)
Chrysanthemum-flowered series (*Helianthus annuus*)
Common Sunflower (*Helianthus annuus*)
Cucumber-leaf Sunflower (*Helianthus debilis*)
Endurance (*Helianthus argophyllus* x *annuus*)
Flore-Pleno (*Helianthus decapetalus* (syn. *H.* x *multiflorus*))
Full Sun (*Helianthus annuus*)
Giant Single (*Helianthus annuus*)
Giant Sunflower (*Helianthus giganteus*)
Giant Sungold (*Helianthus annuus*)
Giant Yellow (*Helianthus annuus*)
Gloriosa Polyheaded (*Helianthus annuus*)

AUTUMN BEAUTY

LEMON QUEEN

CUT FLOWER MIXTURE

PASTICHE

PRADO RED

VELVET QUEEN

Gold and Silver (*Helianthus annuus*)
Happy Face (*Helianthus annuus*)
Helianthus Nuttallii (*Helianthus nuttallii*)
Henry Wilde (*Helianthus hybridus*)
Holiday (*Helianthus annuus*)
Hopi Dye (*Helianthus annuus*)
Incredible (*Helianthus annuus*)
Jumbo (*Helianthus annuus*)
Kid's Stuff (*Helianthus annuus*)
Loddon Gold (*Helianthus decapetalus*
     (*syn. H.* x *multiflorus*))
Mammoth Russian (*Helianthus annuus*)
Maximilian (*Helianthus maximilianii*)
Moonwalker (*Helianthus annuus*)
Naked Sunflower (*Helianthus occidentalis*)
Pacino (*Helianthus annuus*)
Paul Bunyon (*Helianthus annuus*)
Peredovik (*Helianthus annuus*)
Prado Yellow (*Helianthus annuus*)
Prairie Sunflower (*Helianthus petiolaris*)
Russian Giant (*Helianthus annuus*)
Russian Mammoth (Diane's Strain)
     (*Helianthus annuus*)
Saw-tooth Sunflower (*Helianthus grosseserratus*)
Showy Sunflower (*Helianthus* x *laetiflorus*)
Silver Leaf Sunflower (*Helianthus argophyllus*)
Stella (*Helianthus annuus*)
Sun 891 (*Helianthus annuus*)
Sunbeam (*Helianthus annuus*)
Sunbright (*Helianthus annuus*)
Sun Series (*Helianthus annuus*)
Sunspot (*Helianthus annuus*)
Swamp Sunflower (*Helianthus angustifolius*)
Taiyo (*Helianthus annuus*)
Teddy Bear (a.k.a. Golden Globe) (*Helianthus annuus*)
Thin-leaf Sunflower (*Helianthus decapetalus*)
Titan (*Helianthus annuus*)
Tohoku Yae (*Helianthus annuus*)
Willow-leaved sunflower (*Helianthus salicifolius*
     (*syn. H. orgyalis*))
Woodland Sunflower (*Helianthus strumosus*
     (*syn. H. divaricatus*))

ITALIAN WHITE

FULL SUN

GOLD AND SILVER

MOONWALKER

SUNSPOT

TITAN

Index

Credits

PICTURE CREDITS

Sue Atkinson page 44; **Comstock Photo Library** page 9; **Stephen Daniels** page 23 (left); **Kaffe Fassett Design Gallery** page 32 (design: Kaffe Fassett, needlepoint kit production: Ehrman Needlepoint, photography: Debbie Patterson) ; **Mr Fothergill's Seeds Ltd** pages 5 (top), 77, 88, 90, 94, 95; **Garden Answers Magazine** page 40 (top); **Garden/Wildlife Matters** pages 102 (Steffie Shields), 103; **Bob Gibbons** pages 64, 101; **John Glover** pages 41, 47, 65, 68, 75, 84; **Marnie Henderson** page 10; **Insight London Picture Library** pages 51 (Jack Townsend), page 42, 43 (Michelle Garratt); **Park Seed Co.**, Greenwood, SC 29647 pages 82, 93, 96, 98; **Rubber Stampede** page 31; **Derek St Romaine** pages 2, 7, 12, 15, 63, 81, 83; **Graham Strong** pages 19 (left), 20; **Suttons Seeds** pages 23 (right and bottom), 40 (bottom right), 66, 69; **The Garden Picture Library** pages 86, 100 (John Glover), 91, 92 (Mel Watson), 21 (bottom), 97 (Ron Evans), 112 (Juliet Greene); **Thompson & Morgan** pages 4 (top), 16 (right and left), 21 (top), 25 (left), 40 (bottom left), 78, 80 (bottom); **Unwins Seeds Ltd** pages 17, 19 (right).

ACKNOWLEDGEMENTS

The publishers would like to thank the following companies for their kind assistance:
W Atlee Burpee & Co, 300 Park Avenue, Warminster, PA 18974, USA; **Chiltern Seeds**, Bortree Stile, Ulverston, Cumbria LA12 7PB, UK; **Jane Churchill Fabrics and Wallpapers**, 19/23 Grosvenor Hill, London W1X 9HG, UK; **Johnny's Selected Seeds**, Foss Hill Road, Albion, Maine 04910, USA; **Johnsons**, London Road, Boston, Lincolnshire PE21 8AD , UK; **Kaffe Fassett Designs Ltd**, 3 Saville Row, Bath, BA1 2QP, UK; **Mr Fothergill's Seeds**, Kentford, Newmarket, Suffolk, CB8 7QB, UK; **Prairie Nursery**, PO Box 306, Westfield, WI 53964, USA; **Prairie Ridge Nursery**, 9738 Overland Road, Mt Horeb, Wisconsin 53572-2832, USA; **Rubber Stampede**, Unit 8, Ashburton Industrial Estate, Ross-on-Wye, Herefordshire, HR9 7BW, UK and PO Box 246, Berkeley, CA 94701, USA; **Southern Exposure**, PO Box 170, Earlysville, VA 22936, USA; **Seeds of Change**, PO Box 15700, Sante Fe, NM 87506-5700, USA; **Seymour's Selected Seeds**, Admail 962, Farm Lane, Spalding, Lincs, PE11 1TD, UK; **Territorial Seed Company**, PO Box 157, Cottage Grove, OR 97424, USA.

We would also like to thank the following for their help:
Myles Archibald, Elizabeth Dieterle, Eileen Garrett, Sophie Gomm, Julia Green, Simon Henry, Carolyn Hutchinson, Ross Jardine, Brandon Mably, Jenny Macmillan, Polly Powell, Rachel Smyth, Caroline and Adam Stanger and Angela Witherby.

BIBLIOGRAPHY

- *A-Z of Companion Planting*, Pamela Allardice, Cassell, 1993
- *A-Z of Garden Pests and Problems*, Ian G Walls, Treasure Press, 1984
- *Bernard Lavery's Secrets of Giant Sunflowers*, Bernard Lavery, HarperCollinsPublishers, 1996
- *Complete Guide to Flower Arranging*, Jane Packer, Dorling Kindersley, 1995
- *Discovered Dried Flowers*, Christopher Hammond, Hamlyn, 1994
- *Easy Ways with Flower Arranging*, Coral Walker & Jane Forster, Anaya, 1994
- *Flowers for all Seasons: Summer*, Jane Packer, Pavilion/Michael Joseph, 1987
- *Good Ideas for your Garden*, Reader's Digest, 1995
- *Month by Month Organic Gardening*, Lawrence D Hills, Thorsons, 1983
- *Nursery Stencils*, Juliet Moxley, Ebury Press, 1994
- *Reader's Digest A-Z of Perennials*, Reader's Digest, 1992
- *Reader's Digest Color Round the Year*, Reader's Digest, 1990
- *Reader's Digest The Practical Gardener*, Reader's Digest, 1990
- *Stencilling, A Design and Source Book*, edited by Bridget Fraser, Elm Tree Books, 1987
- *The Captured Harvest*, Terence Moore, Cassell, 1983
- *The Companion Garden*, Bob Flowerdew, Kyle Cathie, 1991
- *The Complete Book of Cut Flower Care*, Mary Jane Vaughan, Christopher Helm, 1988
- *The Flower Arranger's Garden*, Rosemary Verey, Conran Octopus, 1989
- *The Flower Arranging Expert*, Dr D G Hessayon, Expert Books, 1994
- *The Good Old-Fashioned Gardener*, Nigel Colborn, Charles Letts & Co., 1993
- *The RHS Gardeners' Encyclopedia of Plants and Flowers*, Dorling Kindersley, 1992
- *The RHS Encyclopedia of Gardening*, Dorling Kindersley, 1992
- *Totally Flowers, Sunflowers*, Joanna Poncavage, Celestial Arts, 1996